THE TEN COMMANDMENTS

Ancient Words ~ Timeless Truth

A Series of Sermons

J. RODMAN WILLIAMS

THE TEN COMMANDMENTS
Ancient Words ~ Timeless Truth
A Series of Sermons
by J. Rodman Williams

Editor: Kathie Muller-Cason

Corinth House Publishers

Kindly direct all inquiries to:
jswms@cox.net

All Scripture quotations, unless otherwise noted, are from the Revised Standard Version of the Bible, (copyright 1946, 1952, 1971. 1973) by the Division of Christian Education of the National Council of Churches of Christ in the United States of America. Used by permission.

All rights are reserved. No part of this book may be reproduced without permission from the publishers except for brief quotations embodied in critical articles and reviews.
All inquiries should be by email.

Cover Image: Courtesy of Jim Munnelly
Author photo: Courtesy of Regent University/CBN

ISBN-13: 978-1481806992
ISBN-10: 1481806998

Copyright © 2012, 2015, Corinth House Publishers.

Published in The United States of America

First Edition

To the Author and Finisher of our faith,
full of Grace and Truth

Table of Contents

The Text of the Ten Commandments   7

Introduction   9

Preface   13

Preamble   17

The First Commandment   19

The Second Commandment   31

The Third Commandment   47

The Fourth Commandment   57

The Fifth Commandment   73

The Sixth Commandment   85

The Seventh Commandment   99

The Eighth Commandment   115

The Ninth Commandment   129

The Tenth Commandment   143

About the Author   157

End Notes   163

The Text of the Ten Commandments

"And God spoke all these words, saying, 'I am the LORD your God, who brought you out of the land of Egypt, out of the house of bondage.

'You shall have no other gods before me.

'You shall not make yourself a graven image, or any likeness of anything that is in heaven above, or that is in the earth beneath, or that is in the water under the earth; you shall not bow down to them or serve them; for I the LORD your God am a jealous God, visiting the iniquity of the fathers upon the children to the third and the fourth generation of those who hate me, but showing steadfast love to thousands of those who love me and keep my commandments.

'You shall not take the name of the LORD your God in vain; for the LORD will not hold him guiltless who takes his name in vain.

'Remember the Sabbath day, to keep it holy. Six days you shall labor, and do all your work; but the seventh day is a Sabbath to the LORD God; in it you shall not do any work, you, or your son, or your daughter, your manservant, or your maidservant, or your cattle, or the sojourner who is within your gates; for in six days the LORD made heaven and earth, the sea, and all that is in them, and rested the seventh day; therefore the LORD blessed the Sabbath day and hallowed it.

'Honor your father and your mother, that your days may be long in the land which the LORD your God gives you.

'You shall not kill.

'You shall not commit adultery.

'You shall not steal.

'You shall not bear false witness against your neighbor.

'You shall not covet your neighbor's house; you shall not covet your neighbor's wife, or his manservant, or his maidservant, or his ox, or his ass; or anything that is your neighbor's.' "

(Exodus 20:1-17)

Introduction

"And God spoke all these words, saying,"

The Ten Commandments have had tremendous influence in the history of mankind. They represent a common moral code accepted by three of the world's great religions: Judaism, Christianity, and Mohammedanism. So widespread has their influence been that an old legend says that when Moses received them they were written in seventy different languages so that they could be quickly and easily distributed throughout all the then known nations of mankind.

In the United States—which is divided religiously into three main bodies, Judaism, Protestantism, and Roman Catholicism—the Ten Commandments act as a unifying force, where rabbi, minister, and priest may speak the same language and have alike moral laws that are unalterably binding. Our three great traditions are all agreed that they are of God and represent moral laws no less valid than physical laws. Human minds, we hold in common, no more created the Ten Commandments than did human minds create the law of gravity. They are laws of God, laws of his moral universe, and to disobey one of the Ten Commandments is to court disaster just as much as, if not more than, to be heedless of the physical law of gravity by casually stepping off a roof-top. On the other hand to obey God's laws, both moral and physical, is to live both spiritually and temporally.

The Ten Commandments are twice listed in the Old Testament: in Exodus 20 and Deuteronomy 5. There is some variation in the wording and content, but the order of the commandments is the same. We shall, in general, follow the wording of Exodus, with occasional references to Deuteronomy.

The numbering system of the Ten Commandments will be the one most generally used in the Protestant tradition. However, it is important to note that there are two major variations: the Jewish, on the one hand, and the Roman Catholic and Lutheran on the other. The Jews think of what we call the "Preamble" as the First Commandment (or First "Word"), and they combine our First and Second Commandment into one. After that the Jewish and general Protestant numbering systems are the same.

The Roman Catholic and Lutheran Churches follow the Jewish system of combining the First and Second Commandment into one; however, they do not think of the "Preamble" as a commandment. Instead, they divide our Tenth commandment into two, which also gives them a complete figure of ten.

Hence, the Roman Catholic-Lutheran numbering system is different throughout from both the Jewish and the general Protestant systems. This is important to bear in mind, for when reference is made to the Third Commandment, for example, it will actually be the Second for Lutherans and Roman Catholics; the Fourth will be the Third, and so on. Roman Catholics have generally used Deuteronomy in quoting the Ten Commandments whereas Luther used the Exodus version.

The Ten Commandments fall naturally into two parts: those concerning man's relation to God and those concerning man's relation to his neighbor. Ordinarily the division is I-IV and V-X. However, since the Fifth Commandment, "Honor your father and your mother," is not exactly concerning one's "neighbor," it might be listed with the first four. The division would then be equal and the nomenclature thus: Commandments I-V concerning man's relation to those *above* him, God and parents, and Commandments VI-X concerning man's relation to those *around* him, his neighbors.

Preface

Before proceeding further into this study, we need to look briefly at the New Testament and recognize:

First, Christ's own teachings concerning the law:

(1) He *reinforces* the law: "Think not that I have come to abolish the law and the prophets: I have come not to abolish them but to fulfill them. For truly, I say to you, till heaven and earth pass away, not an iota, not a dot, will pass from the law[1] until all is accomplished" (Matthew 5:17-18). The words that follow are very strong: "Whoever then relaxes one of the least of these commandments and teaches men so, shall be called least in the kingdom of heaven; but he who does them and teaches them shall be called great in the kingdom of heaven" (verse 19). It would be hard to imagine a stronger reinforcement of the law (commandments).

(2) He *deepens* the law: "You have heard that it was said to the men of old, 'You shall not kill.' But I say to you that every one who is angry with his brother..." (Matthew 5:21-22; see also 5:27-28, 33-34, 38-39, 43-44). The law remains, but Christ proceeds to declare its deeper meaning: the law not only includes the outer action but also the inward intent.

(3) He *summarizes* the law: "You shall love the LORD your God with all your heart, and with all your soul, and with all your

mind. This is the great and first commandment. And a second is like it, you shall love your neighbor as yourself. On these two commandments depend all the law and the prophets" (Matthew 22:37-40).[2] This summary is a drawing together of two Old Testament statements: the first, the love of God, given just after the Decalogue, in Deuteronomy 6:4-5, "Hear, O Israel: The LORD our God is one LORD; and you shall love the LORD your God with all your heart, and with all your soul, and with all your might." The latter, "love of neighbor," is in Leviticus 19:18b: "You shall love your neighbor as yourself." So, without setting aside, or diminishing any of the laws, love is declared to be the motivation on which a true fulfillment of the law depends.

Second, Christ accomplishes several things for those who believe in Him:

(1) He *fulfills* the law in His own life, never departing from the way of righteousness, and so renders vicarious obedience for all who are in Him. Thus is "Christ the end of the law," as the way of righteousness: "Christ is the end of the law for [i.e. 'as the way to'] righteousness to everyone that believeth" (Romans 10:4 KJV). Therefore, they who believe, Israel and mankind at large, are no longer under the law as the way to God's blessing (righteousness, salvation), for Christ has fulfilled it on every man's behalf.

(2) He *redeems* from the curse of the law (a curse because man, in his sinfulness, cannot keep it), by becoming in His death on the cross, a curse for all who believe: "Christ redeemed us from the curse of the law, having become a curse for us" (Galatians 3:13). So does Christ, in His great love, receive the punishment that is our due for the breaking of the law.

(3) He *indwells* those who believe by His Spirit, so that they who walk by faith are enabled, for the first time, to carry out the divine commands (as set forth in the Ten Commandments and by

Christ Himself). Thus, "the just requirement of the law... [may] be fulfilled in us who walk, not according to the flesh, but according to the Spirit" (Romans 8:4). Therefore believers in Christ, no longer under the law as the way of blessing or curse, are enabled by the Spirit of Christ within to fulfill the law's proper and just demands.

Third, the law of God has several functions:

(1) To *declare* God's moral will. That means to set forth clearly what is required of man in relation to God Himself and in relation to one's fellowman. This includes both external action and internal motivation.

(2) To *bring* men to Christ. This is done through the increasing realization that no person, as a sinful human being, can truly keep the law. "The law was our schoolmaster to bring us unto Christ" (Galatians 3:24 KJV).

(3) To serve as a *guide* for Christian living. Believers, no longer under the law, have the law solidly established. "Do we then make void the law through faith? God forbid, yea, we establish the law" (Romans 3:31 KJV). The law, firmly established through faith in Christ and His Spirit within, may at last be fulfilled. The freedom and strength are given to perform God's declared will and purpose.

In the study that follows, we will be explaining the Ten Commandments as God's moral law for all people: Israel, the nations at large, the Christian church, and individual believers. To be sure, there is more to be said about God's will for Israel and the nations than is found in the Decalogue, or even in its summary in the two great commandments. There is much more to be said about God's intention for the church and individual believers than prescriptions of law can possibly contain. However, the underlying conviction of this study is, that by hearing afresh God's moral law again, we may all be called back to those foundational and divine imperatives that can establish us more surely in the way of righteousness and, without which, only destruction looms ahead.

Preliminaries done, let us now proceed, after a brief statement of the "Preamble," to a consideration of the Ten Commandments. Our plan will be that of studying the Commandments one by one and seeking to understand them in the light of Scripture, Old Testament and New Testament. So we shall hope to obey better, and in obeying, live.

Preamble

"I am the LORD your God, who brought you out of the land of Egypt, out of the house of bondage."

This preamble is of vital significance, in that God's commandments are set against the background of His deliverance. God speaks not to slaves, but to free people—people whom He personally has brought "out of the land of Egypt, out of the house of bondage." Therefore, they should be both better able to fulfill God's commands and, at the same time, eager to do so. It is to a free people, grateful for deliverance and now needing guidance for living, that God addresses Himself.

If these commandments speak a living word to the Jew delivered from the bondage of Egypt, how much more do they speak to the Christian delivered from the bondage of evil!

The Ten Commandments are then principles and guides for living to a free people. They are graciously given by God that His people may be warned against the way that leads to destruction, and may always follow the way that leads to life.

The First Commandment

"You shall have no other gods before me."

Many gods have been worshiped by many people throughout the ages. Sometimes these gods have had personal names, such as: Ra, sun-god of Egypt; Baal, fertility-god of Canaan; Marduk, bull-god of Babylon; and Zeus, Greek god of heaven and earth. Sometimes they have been material objects, such as sticks and stones, thought of as containing some divine power within themselves. Sometimes gods have been worshiped without people consciously realizing this worship, as when they have made some human goal their ultimate devotion: such as fame, wealth or pleasure.

This First Commandment, therefore, requires that none of these other gods—these other devotions—come before the LORD God. Indeed, if any "other gods" do come before Him there is no place for God, because worship is being given to that which is less than the true God. There cannot be more than one *God*. If man worships a "god," "God" cannot also be worshiped. If God is truly being worshiped, there is no room left for others.

As a result of this First Commandment, which states the *priority* of God over "other gods," also implies His sole existence. There can be only one God, and no more:

> *"Know therefore this day, and lay it to your heart, that the LORD is God in heaven above and on the earth beneath; there is no other."* (Deuteronomy 4:39)

"You shall have no other gods *before* me" must also mean then, "You shall have no other gods *besides* me."[3]

If we are careful to obey this First Commandment and not "turn aside to the right hand or to the left," what should we do? To answer: *we must see to it that nothing less than God be, or become, our chief goal or highest devotion in life.* The ancient gods mentioned: Ra, Baal, and others), no longer tempt our worship. The worship of supposed powers enclosed in sticks and stones is rare, except among primitive people. Our temptation to the worship of "other gods," therefore, is clearly along the lines already mentioned: fame, wealth, pleasure, and so on. These human satisfactions, when they become the purpose or end of living, are "other gods," and those who pursue them are breaking the First Commandment.

Let us observe some of these "other gods" carefully, and how easily people become their worshipers. These gods might be listed as: Possessions, Pleasure, Prestige, and Power; four "other gods" that vie with the LORD God for worship.

1. Possessions: the accumulation of earthly goods and the devotion to increase of wealth, which may take the place of God.

In this event money, and what money can provide, becomes "Mammon"—the biblical name for any "other god" than the LORD God. Possessions offer earthly security—and since desire for earthly security easily may transcend all else, a person's god may become Mammon.

In the New Testament especially, there are many warnings about this false god Mammon. For one thing, to make the securing of earthly possessions one's goal is *foolish* because, at any time, they may be lost or stolen. "Do not lay up for yourselves treasures on earth, where moth and rust consume and where thieves break in and steal" (Matthew 6:19). For another thing, it is *short-sighted* for, at any moment, death may come, "and the things you have prepared, whose will they be?" (Luke 12:20) Also, even if there were no possible loss on earth (no moths, no thieves) and no death to be faced, possessions are an *unworthy* goal, for "a man's life does not consist in the abundance of his possessions" (Luke 12:15). Furthermore, there is no place for compromise: one cannot with his right hand serve God and his left hand Mammon. "You cannot serve God and mammon" (Matthew 6:24).

Mammon's lure is so subtle that many break the First Commandment in this way without realizing it. Remember the story of the young ruler who came to Jesus with the question, "What must I do to inherit eternal life?" Jesus replied in terms of the commandments having to do with man's relationship to his neighbor, "Do not kill…commit adultery…steal," etc. The young man assured Jesus, "all these things I have observed from my youth." Then Jesus replied, "You lack one thing; go, sell what you have, and give to the poor, and you will have treasure in heaven; and come, follow me." This he was unwilling to do, and "he went away sorrowful; for he had great possessions" (Mark 10:17-22). It was his possessions that stood between him and God, between him and eternal life. He may truly have kept the commandments in relation to his neighbor, but he had broken the First Commandment by placing Mammon above God. Mammon's lure was subtle. Doubtless the young man had always thought of himself as a worshiper of the LORD God, but when the crisis came, an "other god" proved to be his real devotion.

If Mammon is not to be our "other god," we must turn aside neither "to the right hand nor to the left." In some instances, as with the rich young ruler, if Mammon should have a stranglehold, there could be only one procedure: surrender it all, that God might be "God" again.

In other instances, the challenge would not be to surrender, but to stewardship, wherein earthly possessions are used in the service of God. The true steward says: "All that I have is a trust, O LORD, from Thee." Such a one will also say from the heart: "Thy will I shall strive to do, O God, regardless of the cost or the reward."

2. Pleasure: the goal of comfort, the pursuit of contentment, and the search for happiness can take the place of God. Aristotle called it "eudemonia," or "well-being," and made its achievement the basic concern for mankind. This goal is not "pleasure" in a purely physical sense, but in the fullest possible human measure.

Such a person may shun earthly possessions and the Mammon which makes such possible, and look for happiness in the joy of nature, appreciation of the beautiful, love for good books, good music, or good conversation. He may also seek it through travel, hobbies, or recreation of various kinds. On a lower level, he may seek pleasure through satisfaction of physical desires: food, drink, sexual gratification, and so on.

If any of these satisfactions, from the aesthetic to the physical, become a person's chief end in life, they are then "other gods," and he has ceased to worship the LORD God. This is more obvious in the case of physical comforts. Remember the story of the man who said to Jesus, "I will follow you wherever you go." To him Jesus replied, "Foxes have holes, and birds of the air have nests; but the Son of man has nowhere to lay his head" (Luke 9:57-58). Physical comfort could not stand before devotion to God—if so, such a man was worshiping "other gods." The "highest satisfactions" mentioned, just because they are "higher" on the intellectual and aesthetic levels, can be all the more dangerous if they become the highest goals in life. Intellectual pursuit, cultural endeavor, travel, etc., may be "other gods" so engaging one's interests as to replace his final devotion to God.

If the pleasure of aesthetic, intellectual or physical pursuits is not to become "other gods," we must not "turn aside to the right hand or to the left." The right hand might represent the idolatrous devotion already described; the left hand might signify going to the other extreme of denying their value altogether. In between is the "strait and narrow way" where other gods are overcome by placing God and God alone first, seeking to allow His Spirit to pervade and permeate all human endeavors.

Perhaps no figure in the past century symbolized the priority of God and His service over personal pleasure, intellectual attainment, and cultural pursuit, as Albert Schweitzer. Music, philosophy, medicine, theology—any of these could have become his "other god." Instead, he placed all of these at the disposal of the Lord and went as a missionary to the jungles of Africa. Falling neither to "the right hand or to the left," but willingly subordinating the pleasure of earthly attainment to God and His kingdom, he found a life that was rich and full.

3. Prestige: to gain recognition from others, to be popular, to become a "public figure" of repute, can take the place of God.

It will be remembered how Jesus had to chasten His own disciples for their desires in this regard: "A dispute also arose among them, which of them was to be regarded as the greatest" (Luke 22:24). Even after the Resurrection they were still overly concerned about the fortunes of their own nation: "LORD, will you at this time restore the Kingdom to Israel?"

Doing the acceptable thing and acting in the approved manner can very easily become an "other god." "Is it OK to ask God to make me popular?" This may be a question raised by a high school girl and has, of course, a religious reference. Such a question may give evidence that the real god, the real concern, is not the LORD God but an "other god," namely popularity. Unfortunately there are many whose final decisions about social clubs, political parties, vocational services, even church memberships, are made in terms of the most prestige given: which will best help me to "get ahead" in life, which will make people think most highly of me, about which will there be a minimum of criticism for joining?

The tendency to conformity to the local manners may, in a given community, be almost overwhelming. The cause of righteousness may be at stake, but if serious opposition is to be expected, many a person prefers not to bother.

Racial discrimination in restrictive housing and job employment may be a known fact, but far too often people who know about it prefer to remain silent. They might risk their own "reputation" if it became known that they are "crusaders"; so it is far better and safer to go to church on Sunday morning, worship God, and not get too entangled. What "god," however, is really being worshiped? What "god" is calling the signals when the crucial decisions in life are being made? There can only be one answer: it is the "god" of prestige, popularity, and conformity; before this pagan altar the inner spirit is bowed low.

"Crucified under Pontius Pilate," the tragic phrase in the Apostles' Creed, testifies to an act of great evil: the crucifixion of the Son of God by one who permitted the evil to occur. Knowing that Jesus Christ was being unjustly accused, Pilate nevertheless consented, in order that he might stay in the "good graces" of those both above and below him. On the one hand, he did not want Rome think he had let a political traitor go; on the other, he feared to go too far against the prejudice and animosity of the religious leaders around him. Pilate washed his hands of the whole matter, but the washing was an act of false worship: he was bowing low at the altar of the god of "public esteem."

No one can serve God and Prestige any more than one can serve God and Mammon.

God is not a God of Prestige, but of vast humility and condescension. Look now, not at Pontius Pilate but at Jesus Christ, and behold Him, the son of the LORD God, who "made himself no reputation, who even endured the accursed death of the cross."

4. Power: the attainment of authority, the achievement of dominance over people and things, taking the place of God.

History is, of course, filled with examples of those who have lusted for power. Wars beyond measure have been fought by peoples and nations desirous of asserting their authority and achieving dominance over others. People have been enslaved, treaties have been broken, and massacres have occurred because of the intense desire to overcome, subjugate, and exercise domination. Kings have fought kings, rulers have warred against rulers, priests have fought priests, politicians have tried to unseat politicians and business and industrial leaders have engaged in fierce combat. The drive behind much of this has been, and continues to be, the lust for power.

So it is that husbands and wives have divorced, parents and children been pulled apart, and employers and employees at bitter odds; again so frequently because of the drive for power and authority. A husband who must dominate his wife, a parent who must rule over the life of his child now an adult, and an employer who must show "who's the boss" at every turn. The result is tragedy and misery all around. Somehow no other goal, no other god, seems to possess people with quite such intensity. It is an evil of proportions, seemingly, beyond all others.

In this regard, it is highly significant that the biblical picture of the devil, Satan, is of one who is the very incarnation of the lust for power; seeking and claiming it for himself and tempting others to strive for the same. In Genesis, the serpent's temptation is to power: "You will be like God (or "as gods")," Genesis 3:5. In the Gospels the story is the same; Satan, claiming this power, offers it to Christ: "...(he) showed him all the kingdoms of the world in a moment of time, and said to him, 'To you I will give all this authority and their glory; for it has been delivered to me, and I give it to whom I will. If you, then, will worship me, it shall all be yours' " (Luke 4:5-7).

"All this authority and their glory": all claimed for oneself, all sought for oneself, all prized so dearly as to be worshiped, and you shall have it. Such power as the goal of life is the devil's own way, and to seek it is to bow down and worship at the very throne of Satan. It follows, then, that of all the "other gods" that men may worship, none is more fiendish than the god of power: for such a god is the final evil.

We must constantly, therefore, be on the alert for manifestations of this evil genius in ourselves. However much we may have dedicated our lives to the service of God and humanity, there come moments when we are tempted to seek authority over others, to make claims for ourselves (or to feel them inwardly); and in achieving position or prominence, to use that very situation to exert power over others. It is quite often the "good" people, those who earnestly seek to live for the Kingdom of God, who are most severely tried by this evil genius. Why is this? Because in their very dedication the genuine power of God begins to operate in their lives, and *this very power becomes an occasion for temptation.* Was not this true of Jesus Himself? If true of Him, how much more any one of us! What can someone do to fight this dreaded evil? We should not strive against having power, for there is no merit in weakness itself; but we should strive mightily against the will to dominate, the will to rule over others. Devotion to such fiendish power is "devil-worship," and the only way we can be sure of driving away this evil is to do what Jesus Christ did. Rather than allowing the temptation to press Him further, He immediately repelled it by saying, "You shall worship the LORD your God, and Him only shall you serve" (Luke 4:8).

The continuing worship of God, the constantly renewed commitment of ourselves to the LORD—moment by moment, hour by hour, day by day—can help keep us from being part of that dark evil that holds the world in its dominion. Most of all, we have to stay close to Christ, for He was both tempted to worship at the throne of evil power, and overcame that difficult temptation. In the simple and beautiful words of Hebrews 2:18: "Because He Himself has suffered and been tempted, He is able to help those who are tempted."

"You shall have no other gods before me." The other gods are all around. Four have been named who call for our worship: not Ra, Baal, Marduk, or Zeus, but Possessions, Pleasure, Prestige, and Power. To bow before them is to forsake the LORD God and to forgo life that is abundant and full. To have "no other gods," before or besides Him, is truly to have all things.

Notes and Meditation:

The Second Commandment

"You shall not make for yourself a graven image, or any likeness...."

Let us begin by inquiring into the meaning of His Second Commandment and the reason for its being given. *What*, first of all, *is prohibited* in this commandment?

There have been interpreters who believed that the Second Commandment forbids any kind of figurative art. Painting and sculpture, on any level, from childish representations of a few marks or a little clay to that of the great painters and sculptors, all is forbidden. If the art seeks to image anything "in heaven above...earth beneath, or...in the water under the earth," then it violates the Second Commandment. This, then, would refer not just to images of God, but images of anything that exists.

The above, however, cannot be the meaning of the commandment, for Exodus records this commandment not only in Exodus 20, but also in Exodus 25-28. Here there are commandments to make: cherubim (representing heavenly creatures) of gold, a lampstand with hammered work of flowers, and a robe for Aaron decorated with pomegranates. Artwork, therefore, is surely not forbidden.

The true meaning, rather, is that *man shall not make any graven image as an attempt to represent God*. This is clear from the second

31

portion of the Commandment beginning, "...You shall not bow down to them or serve them." Cherubim, flowers and pomegranates were not intended to represent God, and therefore are proper; but any sculptural figure ("graven image"), or painting ("likeness") of anything that would seek to give God some form—celestial, terrestrial, human, or sub-human—is taboo.

The complete commandment, therefore, is: first, no representations of God; second, no bowing down to them or serving them. Put even more simply: no images of God and no image worship or idolatry.

What is the reason for this two-fold prohibition?

First, let us consider the making of images of God not allowed. No image of God should be made, first of all, because *such detracts from His living reality*. Immediately at the conclusion of giving the Ten Commandments, God says to Moses:

> *"Thus you shall say to the people of Israel: 'You have seen for yourselves that I have talked with you from heaven. You shall not make gods of silver to be with me, nor shall you make for yourselves gods of gold.'"* (Exodus 20:22-23)

"You have seen for yourselves that I have talked with you"; God was at that moment tremendously real, and surely no image could represent Him. He had spoken from heaven, the realm of the spiritual, not the material. And He had also spoken to them on earth, as they knew, for "all the people perceived the thunderings and the lightnings and the sound of the trumpet and the mountain smoking" (Exodus 20:18). God was terrifyingly real ("let not God speak to us, lest we die" (Exodus 20:19); far too much so for any image to approximate His reality.

Second, how could He be imaged? Should He be given a physical form when He is in heaven, and when on earth He is present in fire and cloud? Should He be given a mouth when His voice is that of thunder and trumpet blast? There is nothing to image, and therefore *any material representation distorts His very nature.* God is spiritual—and so cannot be represented by anything tangible.

Silver and gold may indeed be among the finest of earth's treasures, but even the most precious materials of earth, molded into some shape to represent the divine, are both a detraction from God's living reality and a distortion of His very nature.

It is not the fact that such images may lead to idolatry that makes them wrong in the first instance, but that they do not lead to God.

Because of their tangible nature they are barriers to His reality; and because of their fixed-form they compress God into a small entity. God, who is spiritual, cannot be expressed in material.

In the New Testament Paul expressed this spirituality of God, and the impossibility of the material representing Him, by saying: "He (God) is not far from each one of us, for 'In Him we live and move and have our being'....we ought not to think that the Deity is like gold, or silver, or stone, a representation by the art and imagination of man" (Acts 17:27-29). God is not *like* anything that human art or imagination can devise—and therefore attempting falls into error.

It ought to be clear that the Scripture by no means declares that art has no place in the worship of God. God is to be worshiped in "the beauty of holiness"; therefore artistic representations of many things in heaven, on earth, and under the earth may be very helpful.

Why would numerous flowers, pomegranates, and cherubim be *commanded* by God for the tabernacle service if these artistic works were not of value in bringing one closer to His presence? Therefore, we may be sure that churches containing stained glass windows, mosaics, carved altar pieces, crosses, and so on—if these are beautifully and reverently done—may be true sanctuaries for the realization of the presence of the Divine. The only, and absolute, prohibition is that nothing made by human hands seek to portray God Himself.

Again call to mind the tabernacle services. Nothing is more significant than the fact that, though candlestick and cherubim might help one in the worship of God, nothing humanly contrived finally represented God Himself. There was the ark of the covenant, with its mercy seat underneath and the cherubim on each side and above; but it was from the emptiness *above* the mercy seat and *between* the two cherubim that the voice of God spoke:

"There I will meet with you, and from above the mercy seat, from between the two cherubim that are upon the ark of testimony, I will speak." (Exodus 25:22)

The way then to the true worship of God leads through the beauty of the earthly to the holiness of the Eternal. *But*, no attempt may be made to represent the Eternal Himself.

Therefore, to think in terms of modern church rather than ancient tabernacle, any image of God Himself is forbidden. Roman Catholicism is often criticized for its many images of Christ; as on the cross, the altar, the Twelve Stations of the Cross, and sometimes images of God the Father—and the criticism is just. But Protestantism likewise also errs, through its images of the Divine: in stained glass windows, paintings of Christ above the chancel, carvings of Jesus with His disciples on the Communion Table, and so on. As pious as the intention may be that brings such divine imagery into the sanctuary, it is a breach of the Second Commandment. God simply cannot be worshiped "in *spirit* and truth," John 4:24, because the imagery with its fixed form detracts from and even distorts His presence.

The arguments, of course, are strong and sometimes heated that such imagery need not be a handicap to worship, but instead may be a medium for divine-human encounter. A Roman Catholic praying before a crucifix, beholding the graven image of Christ's tortured body, feels the reality of Christ's suffering and death. A Protestant worshiping, either at church or home, with a likeness of Christ at hand, feels the reality of Christ's living presence. Why then are not both aids to worship? Do they not become media of the Spirit? The answer again must be that such a "graven image" and such a "likeness" are wrong because the reality of God, who is spirit, is *always* diminished through any non-spiritual, therefore material, attempt to represent Him. It is not that an image-using Roman Catholic and Protestant do not worship at all—for God always rewards those who diligently seek Him—but their worship is badly handicapped at whatever point the image comes into focus. *At that point* worship cannot be "in spirit and truth." If they worship truly, it is in spite of, not because of, the representations of the divine.

The argument continues: but was not Christ Himself the corporeal, tangible, material representation of the Divine? Was not He the incarnate, therefore flesh and blood presence of God Almighty? The answer is "Yes." Well then, why not continue to give Him corporeal reality through crucifixes, paintings, and the like? If it was important that Christ should reveal God in the flesh, visibly to the eye, why is it not perfectly proper, even important, to continue that revelation as best we can through image and likeness?

First, to answer this question: is it not highly unusual that so much should have been written about Jesus Christ in the New Testament without a single attempt to describe His appearance? We do not have the *slightest* statement about His height, color of hair or body build—absolutely nothing of how He *looked*. Was it because the writers did not know, or was it because they knew, or sensed, what would happen if any description *were given*? The answer is surely the latter, for immediately people would want to fashion images and likenesses, and this would become more important than hearing God's Word spoken through Him. So, no description is given; and therefore all images since then are utter figments of the imagination, and completely at variance with the intentions of the New Testament writers.

Furthermore—and this is vastly important—any bodily portrayal of the Son of God cannot possibly aid in worship, because Christ, since His Ascension, is no longer present corporeally. He is present in a far richer way, namely, in the Holy Spirit. Christ left His disciples *bodily* so that He might be present with His church *spiritually*: and so He is and continues to be. Like the presence of God in the tabernacle, God is so real that nothing visible could portray Him. So is Jesus Christ in His Church. Mercy seat and heavenly cherubim, Holy Table, and Holy Cross, all prepare for His Presence. Now when God speaks, and thereby reveals Himself, it is "above" and "between," it is "in, with, and under" all things physical: for God in Christ is the living Spirit.

But, one argues again: people *need* crucifixes and pictures, if for nothing else as a constant reminder of the reality of the Divine. It is fine and good to talk about God's spiritual presence, but people generally are quite unspiritual; therefore some images may make them able to turn their thoughts to more serious matters. Therefore for church, home, hospital, or school—where ever you will—to have "good" representations of Christ around *could help* lead in the right direction.

The answer must be: there is *no* representation of the Divine that is "good." Therefore: however much a crucifix or picture may turn one's thoughts in a "serious" direction, those thoughts cannot discover God; *for the religious image both speaks of God and denies Him at the same time.* The image says: "Behold your God"; but when someone looks, what he sees is the contrary of God. This is because the picture is finite, God is infinite; the picture is material, God is spiritual; the picture is particular, God is universal.

The God of the image is *not* God; however just, loving, or holy He may be made to appear. It is rather the contradiction of God, and therefore cannot represent His reality. Far better to have no image at all than to have one *seem* to lead to God but end by barring His presence. Images of the divine can never, therefore, be a help to anyone because they promise much and give nothing.

Sadly, for how many people, the reality of the living Christ is again and again frustrated by pictures of Him in bodily form. The Christ they see is the Christ of the crucifix, the Christ of some artist's imagination; they can never really see Christ. He cannot get through to them because there is always some image of Him standing in their way.

Indeed, not only do images of the Divine offer no help to His presence, but just as surely as they seem to be a way to His reality, they are *a great evil*. The image that beckons, deludes; the picture that promises so much help, frustrates; but also, the image-user may be deceived into thinking that such cannot be the case. If he does admit that he has not gotten very far yet, he still wants to believe that some day God will become real, through its continued use.

The image, for all its seeming good, is, therefore, a vicious evil. Like some great idol it offers much, but gives nothing; it offers again, and those who have received nothing hope again, only to have that hope frustrated. It offers again and again, and those who are now hopeless are in its power and cannot find the living God.

No other than a radical solution will help, therefore. *Images of the Divine should be done away with.* They cannot be "improved" by having let us say, a more "holy" Christ, a more "virile appearing" one, or a more "appealing one." All the "mores" only add up to the same impossibility, the same frustration, and the same evil. The Divine is not to be imaged because the Divine cannot be; and all attempts are doomed to failure and destruction.

Images of the Divine should go! Like any idol they can be quickly destroyed; but also like any idol, if they are left standing, they destroy those who use them. Only when the Divine images go, will God come: and again there can be the worship of Him in spirit and truth.

A word of caution is necessary, however: do not let anyone become so anti-icon as to think that *all* images must be destroyed! The story is a grim one indeed: the way reformers have, during certain periods, stripped churches of every worship aid and object, thinking that the only way to obey the Second Commandment was to get rid of all religious imagery, so that there might be little more than a room with four bare walls and a plain ceiling. Sacred paintings, stained glass windows and religious symbolism—all were destroyed. The intent: the purification of worship through the removal of all worship aids.

Doubtless, many reformers felt the evil of divine imagery to be so woven into almost everything, that moderation was well nigh impossible, hence: a clean sweep.

Maybe there was no other way than revolution; be that as it may, the result was surely not ideal. "Impoverished" worship may be some improvement on "impure" worship, since there is no longer a false image of the Divine. However, just as surely as it is impoverished, it may be little worship at all.

God is not to be worshiped *falsely*; but He *is* to be worshiped. Do not let the zeal to keep the Second Commandment prevent anyone from knowing the God who gave it.

Therefore, we now come to the other extreme of those who seek to worship God in stark simplicity. They build churches like auditoriums, with not even a suggestion of the Divine about them; except perhaps a Bible on a pulpit. There is no beauty of color, no loveliness of window, no religious symbolism: not even a plain cross. The cherubim, lamp stand, and robe of the old tabernacle are completely forgotten and nothing fills the void. The atmosphere is frequently little more than that of a public gathering place, in which God may often be mentioned, but no one is really aware of His presence.

The result: rather than the worship of God in spirit and truth, He is hardly worshiped at all.

This, of course, is not to say that the worship of God is dependent upon tangible aids. One can worship God in the barest of rooms, or in no room at all; one can worship anywhere and at anytime, for "in Him we live and move and have our being." Indeed, there are moments when quite unexpectedly—perhaps even in a non-religious setting—God becomes quite real and a person does worship inwardly. God is free and can reveal Himself when and where He wills. However, at the same time, one must quickly add that though God is not dependent on tangible forms we, as human beings, are creatures and ordinarily need forms and symbols to arrive at the Eternal.

There are those who believe that God may be worshiped better when all of creation is excluded from the experience. The five senses, they say, are 'handicaps,' since they make one aware of the external world. Therefore, to worship truly is no longer to see, hear, touch, smell, or taste—but turning inward, to allow one's inner spirit to make contact with the Divine. "Let sense be dumb, let flesh retire" that God may descend upon the heart. This, however, is *a denial of our creatureliness.* God will descend upon the human being and the "spirit with spirit can meet," but ordinarily it comes via the organs of perception He has given us. He did not give us these senses to meditate other reality, and then suddenly to become "dumb" before Him. It is when *all* the senses are alert and eager for the Divine that He may be most easily and truly received.

Then what, we are now ready to ask, is the situation in which the worship experience may ordinarily be at its highest? The answer:

It is that situation in which, avoiding all divine imagery, material aids may be a medium for the Divine-human encounter.

The sanctuary does not have to be an ornate cathedral, but it should be filled with *beauty*: beauty of construction and equipment, of religious symbolism, of song and prayer, of all things which the eyes behold, the ears hear, and the other senses experience. It should be filled with the beauty of *holiness*: the whole service should bring the worshiper, through hymn and prayer, Scripture and sermon, closer to the presence of the Living God. After robe and ritual, lamp stand and cherubim, there may come the voice of the LORD, who speaks from eternity.

To summarize so far: we began by noticing that the Second Commandment forbids: first, the making of divine images, and second, image worship. We inquired as to the reason for this prohibition and have, until now, considered only the question of image making. We have seen that any imaging of the divine distracts and distorts from His reality and proves, finally, to be a barrier to true worship. What has not been stressed yet is that *divine images may also lead to image worship or idolatry*—the second thing prohibited in the Second Commandment.

Let it be repeated that *divine imagery is wrong even if it does not lead to idolatry. It is wrong in the first instance, because it does not lead to God.* This is important to stress again, because there are those who defend divine imagery on the thesis that it does not *necessarily* lead to idolatry, and if it does not, then the imagery is right and proper. Such a defense is off base because it fails to recognize that all divine imagery is wrong. This is true, prior to any consideration of the matter of idolatry.

Now, having twice repeated the point about the basic evil of divine imagery, one must recognize the further fact that such imagery may, and often does, indeed lead to idolatry. In Egypt, for example, at the time of the Exodus, this shift from image making to idolatry had taken place long before. Animals that had begun merely as images setting forth the divine, or various aspects of the divine, themselves became objects of veneration and worship. It is against this background that one may very well appreciate the story of the golden calf, and Israel's idolatry. The Israelites, whatever their devotion to God, had all their lives in Egypt breathed the very atmosphere of idol-worship. So, even though they had at last been set free from Egypt, and had seen the mighty hand of God at work in their deliverance, there was still a strong pull from the old gods. The result: it took only a few days or weeks of Moses' separation from them, up on the mountain, to make them feel deserted by the LORD God, and to embrace idolatry: "Up, make us gods [they cried to Aaron], who shall go before us. And he...made a molten calf; and they said, 'These are your gods, O Israel, who brought you up out of the land of Egypt!' " This, then, was a drastic breaking of the Second Commandment. It was for them not even a case of slipping from imagery into idolatry, that had already happened in Egypt, and so they became idolaters directly. They made a graven image with the deliberate, intentional, and avowed purpose of worshiping it.

Let us return briefly now to considering the way, as with the Egyptians, that divine imagery so easily slips into idolatry. The image, at the outset, may merely be a figure representing God or some god, but, as time goes by, it is almost inevitable that the image becomes increasingly identified with the divine. The image can be seen day in and day out, but the god, or God, cannot. Who knows whether the god is even there when one worships and prays, but his image surely is, so why not pray directly to the image? So imagery soon becomes idolatry, and the creature—created by man—becomes the object of worship rather than the Creator.

In our Judeo-Christian tradition, with its constant warnings against idolatry (both Old and New Testaments are violently opposed to it) and its insistence on the spirituality of God, idolatry is seldom an obvious activity *within* religion itself.

In the Old Testament, idolatry within the faith of Israel is practically non-existent. There is indeed an abundance of it in reference to other gods (those of Egypt, Canaan, Mesopotamia, etc.), but rare was the Hebrew who would dare make a graven image of the LORD God. The Second Commandment rang too loudly in his ears, and God was just too exalted for anyone to image. Therefore, with no graven images of God, idolatry within their faith was ruled out.

As stated, the Christian faith, likewise, has firmly opposed idolatry; but because the same stress has not always been given to the Second Commandment regarding graven images, idolatry—for all attempts to the contrary—has inevitably, though not always admittedly, crept in. In Roman Catholicism this has been especially true. The Christ of the crucifix, the Christ of the "bleeding heart," and the Christ carrying the cross at the various "stations"—all of these images, seen again and again and bowed before, cannot help but come to represent power and meaning in themselves. It is even within the Roman Catholic view of "transubstantiation," where the bread and wine—formerly symbols of Christ's presence—are said to become quite literally His body and blood.

For the Roman Catholic, transubstantiation is a fact: he actually believes that the finite can contain the infinite and therefore "idolizes" the Sacrament. He cannot help bringing the same spirit into all his worship, constantly tending to worship the material object. Theologically, the Roman Catholic is only justified in doing this with the bread and wine, but actually—for all the theological denials to the contrary—he does it with many objects: from Christ down through Mary, Joseph, and innumerable saints. In Roman Catholicism, therefore, idolatry has won a theological victory in the case of the Sacrament: *it is proper to worship the material object.* It has also won a practical victory on innumerable fronts, when the worshiper makes little or no distinction between the image and the idolatry of it.

Protestantism, however, is not void of idolatry either. There may be no theological justification for it—as with "transubstantiation"—nor are there quite as many images around. However, such divine imagery as the Protestant does use: pictures and carvings, especially of Christ, easily becomes the practical center of devotion, and though he would not ordinarily admit it in theory, in practice he may soon begin to worship the Christ of the image rather than Christ present in the Holy Spirit.

All imagery of the Divine, therefore, actually has within itself the power both to *distort and to dominate.* On the one hand, it distorts and denies the presence of God—as we have noted at length—and then having, so to speak, gotten God out of the way, it tends to dominate and demean. What began as a pious image ends as an impious idol—and God, first denied, is finally replaced by an object belonging to His own creation.

If the earlier statement was true: that all divine imagery should be put away because of its obstruction of the Divine, how doubly true, when in addition to that obstruction, is the inevitable occurrence of idolatry! The result is so tragic: *the God who must be worshiped* if man is to live truly and abundantly, has not only been shut off, He has been replaced by an idol of Himself.

"You shall not make for yourself a graven image, or any likeness...." In conclusion: to seek to image the Divine is to commit a heinous sin. True it is a subtle one, because the imagery may be done from a seemingly high-minded desire to give expression to the nature of the Eternal. What more worthy of art than to seek to make the Divine real? And yet the very attempt is both impossible and wrong: for God Himself cannot, and will not, be subjected to even the highest of human objectification. Artistic representations, for all their beauty, make the Creator into a creature; He is no longer the Infinite and Eternal One. It is a grievous sin against the Creator to seek to set Him forth in imagery that cannot help but make Him seem finite and temporal—a figure, who though standing above creation however the artist may portray Him, is, nonetheless and of necessity, pictured in creaturely fashion.

Such imagery is a sin against God, and finally—as we have pointed out repeatedly—is a grievous sin against man. Man is made so that the highest goal and the greatest need of his life is to worship God. Worship God and you shall live is the basic theme of faith. How is God to be worshiped? As He is, namely, Spirit—for "God is Spirit"—and it follows that "those who worship Him must worship Him in spirit and truth." Imagery of the divine, because it "de-spiritualizes," is, therefore, a barrier to worship: it detracts and distorts and, having objectified the spiritual, tends toward idolatry. The image so dominates the mind that the worshiper finds himself worshiping the visible; and even though he desires to get "beyond" to the spiritual, he cannot help but project the image yet further and further. So does man worship no God but a human image, and such worship is idolatrous. God has vanished; the image is enthroned, and man cannot find the way to His Creator.

Divine imagery is a grievous sin against man because it prevents him from fulfilling his highest goal and greatest need: to worship God.

How vastly important is the Second Commandment! To disobey it is immeasurable sin against both God and man; to obey it is to make possible true worship of the Eternal.

Notes and Meditation:

The Third Commandment

"You shall not take the name of the LORD your God in vain; for the LORD will not hold him guiltless who takes His name in vain."

In order to appreciate the meaning and significance of this commandment, let us first notice the interesting fact that God has a special name: the "LORD." In reading the Third Commandment we may too easily assume the "LORD" and "God" are the same; however, the former is written with four capital letters, indicating something special in this particular title for the Deity.

Exodus 3 contains the story of this special name of God: as the "LORD." God tells Moses that He intends to deliver His people from their Egyptian oppression. Also, that Moses is to go to the Israelites and say that the God of their fathers has designated him to lead them out of Egypt. At this point, Moses said to God: "If I come to the people of Israel and say to them, 'The God of your fathers has sent me to you' and they ask me, 'What is his name?' What shall I say to them?"

God replies to Moses: "I AM WHO I AM." And He said, "Say this to the people of Israel, 'I AM has sent me to you.'" God also said to Moses, "Say this to the people of Israel, 'The LORD, the God of your fathers, the God of Abraham, the God of Israel, and the God of Jacob, has sent me to you: this is my name forever, and thus I am to be remembered throughout all generations.'"

"I AM" and "LORD" are obviously synonymous terms: the word "LORD" standing for the four Hebrew letters "YHWH" in this passage. The name "YHWH," or "LORD," is God's special name "forever...throughout all generations." Incidentally, this name of God is sometimes written in English as "Yahweh."[4]

Much to the point of this Third Commandment is the way in which we have come to use the word "LORD" for "YHWH." The Jewish people, for fear of breaking the commandment, would not dare even to pronounce the name of God. It was too dangerous to do, because they might "take it in vain." Therefore, instead of saying "Yahweh," they came to substitute another word more equivalent to our English word "LORD." They would read "YHWH" silently, but on their lips it became "LORD."

Actually then, our English translations, which put the commandment as "You shall not take the name of the LORD your God in vain," represent *in the very translation* the traditional concern of keeping the commandment by not lightly using "Yahweh." We even write it as LORD. So, from the ancient Jewish viewpoint, we are on even safer ground than they were. They read it in Scripture but refused to say it; we neither read it nor say it, since it is not in our Scripture at all!

The Third Commandment traditionally, then, has led to much concern about the sacredness of the Divine Name. Exodus 3, which gives the story of the Divine Name also tells, prior to that event, of God speaking to Moses out of the burning bush and impressing upon him the Divine Holiness:

> *"Do not come near; put off your shoes from your feet, for the place on which you are standing is holy ground."* (Exodus 3: 1-6)

If God is holy, then surely the Name is holy also. If one should not "come near" to the Divine Presence, then he needs to be equally careful about the Divine Name. It is proper to say that a basic concern of the Third Commandment is the holiness of God. Our reverence for Him is clearly demonstrated by the way in which we use His holy name.

Do we use it in a profane or reverent manner?

Another translation of the Bible puts the Third Commandment this way: "You shall not use the name of the Eternal, your God, profanely; for the Eternal will not acquit anyone who uses His name profanely."[5]

If we wish to obey the Third Commandment and therefore "live," we must not profane the name of the Eternal, the LORD our God.

To obey the Third Commandment would mean, first: in religious activities such as worship and prayer, Scripture reading and pious conversation, we must avoid taking God's name in vain. Indeed, it is within the context of religion itself, that this commandment may be broken most seriously. Does this mean then that one must avoid the *use* of God's name—in whatever its expressions: "LORD," "Jehovah, "Yahweh," "the Eternal," etc.? The answer must be "No"—however much we may respect the Jewish person who tries not to speak God's name at all, and however much our translation of "YHWH" into "LORD" also has been influenced by tradition.

We are not told that the name of "YHWH," or "LORD," is not to be used at all, but that when used, is not to be taken vainly or profanely. The real violation of the Third Commandment in religious acts, therefore, is that of using God's name in a light, empty, or thoughtless fashion.

Perhaps nobody sins quite as greatly, in this point, as the Sunday morning worshiper in church. By the very nature of the worship service, God's name is frequently used: through hymns, unison prayer, responsive reading, creed, and other parts of the service. To use God's name thoughtlessly, in any of these ways, is to take it "in vain." One of our hymns points to this danger with the line, "In vain we tune our formal songs."[6] This means to honor God with our lips, while our hearts are still far from Him.

Of course, such vanity in worship is not limited to the church service, but may be carried on elsewhere; for example, in the home. "Grace" at meals, family prayers, even private devotions, can sometimes become empty and routine. These religious acts, so filled with wondrous possibilities of divine grace and Christian growth, may—unless care is given—easily slip into the sin of taking God's name in vain.

Conversations about the "things of God" carried on by people: whether on the level of theologians or laymen may, through the casual use of God's name, share in the breach of God's law. To speak of God in the same manner as one would of some human being, or with as little reflection as is given to any passing idea, is surely to take God's name in vain.

Since it is so very easy to slip in this regard, what is the person to do who wants to obey God's law? Let him go neither to the right hand nor to the left: the right hand of trying not to use God's name at all for fear of misusing it, the left hand of not really caring too much and therefore indulging in vanity. In between is the right way of seeking earnestly, at all times, to say the name of God in a reverent and devout spirit.

This means, as one example, better preparation for worship so that when the name of God *is used* there is true reverence. To arrive at church at the last minute, if not later, without a prayer being said ahead of time—with no heart-searching or no yearning for worship "in spirit and in truth"—such action is almost certain to lead to a breaking of the Third Commandment.

As always, in the breaking of God's Commandment, one hurts one's self also, for such poor worship makes for poverty of soul. The name of God and the presence of God, which make for abundant living, is lost, and one goes away empty, having missed the indwelling and infilling of the Divine.

Obedience to the Third Commandment means, secondly: *the avoiding of all profane use of God's name in common speech.* If the breach of the Commandment is most serious in religious matters, we do not mean to imply that "profanity"—in the commonly accepted sense of the term—is a light matter.

Profanity is indeed *a sad and dreary business.* It is the use of the Divine Name: God, LORD, Christ, and so on, not as an act of worship, not as a topic of sincere conversation, but as a means to some human end: to express strong emotional feeling such as surprise, anger, or disgust.

Profanity is a vicious evil because, in its indulgence, God is no longer God; the One who stands before and above all else. His name is tossed around vainly to express one's own self-centered feelings. In profanity, God becomes one's servant, and God's name one's own petty tool.

One of the gravest tragedies resulting from profanity is its tendency to make worship and prayer a virtual impossibility. The profane person cannot look up to the name of God with reverence and awe; it only makes him think of swearing. The name of Jesus cannot be solemnly used for it becomes a common oath, and to hear a prayer close with some such phrase as "for Christ's sake" is to create a mood of frustration. The argument is sometimes advanced that profanity is not *really* evil because it is simply a thoughtless habit with many people. The answer: is not anything evil which will not permit the worship of God "in spirit and truth"?

Profanity is *a confession of inner weakness.* People not really knowing God, or the true strength that comes from worship and prayer, may try to appear strong and bold by presuming to use the Divine name at will. The weak person, not really sure of himself or of what he says, tries to convince himself, and others through strong language. Actually he convinces nobody, and only fools himself. Profanity and words are cheap, and soon nobody knows what to believe.

Remember the words of Jesus:

"Do not swear at all, either by heaven, for it is the throne of God, or by the earth for it is His footstool, or by Jerusalem, for it is the city of the great King. And do not swear by your head, for you cannot make one hair white or black. Let what you say be simply 'Yes' or 'No'; anything more than this comes from evil."

(Matthew 5:34-37)

These words may refer primarily to an oath to perform a certain duty to God, but surely they also apply in all situations where swearing of any kind may occur. Jesus is saying that trying to strengthen one's speech by adding any force to it from the outside is evil.

A man's "Yes" should mean "Yes," and if it does not, he should not swear to make it seem to do so. Who is the person that is most respected? Invariably it is he who speaks simply and whose word is his bond.

Profanity, again, is *a kind of desperate substitute for prayer.* Human beings are made to pray and, therefore, to invoke the name of God. Man is by nature a "praying animal." Consequently, if he fails to use the name of God in a worshipful manner, he may feel constrained to use it vainly. Profanity then is a kind of "inverted praying." Man must pray and, if he does not call upon God sincerely, God's name will be used some other way.

A man so profane in speech as to disturb many other people around him was suddenly brought to his senses by a friend who, not able to bear it any longer, said quietly to him, "Why don't you stop your praying?" The shock of hearing his profanity labeled as "praying" was so strong that he immediately stopped the practice. God could no longer be the servant of his whims and strong feelings; the profane man finally had to find a way back to God through worship and prayer.

To obey the Third Commandment means, finally, *to take the name of the LORD seriously: to live for Him and His name, and not for one's own.* To break the Third Commandment is not to take God's name upon oneself, but to live for one's own name instead.

Every person who calls himself a Christian has taken upon himself the name of the LORD. In the baptismal ceremony the person is baptized "in the name of the Father, and of the Son, and of the Holy Spirit." If the one baptized is a child, the parents promise to bring him up in the nurture and admonition of the LORD, and if the one baptized is of age, he must himself always seek to keep the name of the LORD above his own.

What a tragedy if parents bring up their baptized children in an atmosphere where the family name and reputation, or the child's name and advancement, become more important than the name of the LORD! What a grievous evil if a young person or adult, after taking the name of Christ, is still more concerned about himself than God and His purposes! Such people, however solemn the religious acts, have taken the name of the LORD their God in vain.

To keep the Third Commandment means *to come and go in the name of the LORD and not in one's own name.* David standing before Goliath and saying, "You come to me with a sword and with a spear and with a javelin; but I come to you in the name of the LORD of hosts" (1 Samuel 17:45), represents magnificently one who sets the LORD's name above his own and comes and goes in that name. So it was with Jesus Christ Himself; for it was of Him that the multitudes cried, "*Blessed be he who comes in the name of the LORD*" (Matthew 21:9). Surely these words apply to all who take the LORD's name in such wondrous fashion.

A person who has no need to boast of himself but whose strength, pride and joy are in the LORD isn't only richly blessed in his own life but is also a benediction to others. There is a radiancy, an outspokenness, and a concern for all people stemming from his commitment to God, which makes him like a refreshing stream flowing into the lives of others. Since he doesn't come in his own name but the Name of the LORD, he is not introverted but extroverted; he is not ego-centered but other-centered. The world is expansive around him—and the world rejoices in his presence.

Tragically the world suffers greatly from the vast number of those who do not come "in the name of the LORD," and who therefore take His name in vain. Indeed, they may talk of the LORD, call Him by name, and even offer prayers to Him, but they are no abiding blessing because they are still coming in their own names. Always jockeying for position, they are sensitive about their own ideas, defensive if anyone dare criticize, cuddling their egos as if they were infants in arms, and if their names are spoken immediately, porcupine-like, all a-bristle to be sure that what is said is favorable: and, if not, to thrust their quills into the awful offender. They have taken the LORD's name in vain. The only name that really matters is their own.

The world, however, is sick and tired of observing those taking the LORD's name in vain, blowing their own trumpets. When at last it sees someone like David or Christ, not coming in their own name, hosannas will echo across the mountain-tops and through the valleys, palm branches will wave in glad tribute, while even the stones of the earth are longing to cry out in sheer ecstasy. For truly the whole creation longs for the manifestation of the sons of God—those who come not in their own name but in the name of the LORD.

"You shall not take the name of the LORD your God in vain": through false worship, profanity, or living for one's own name. Let us seek to live only for God's glory.

Notes and Meditation:

The Fourth Commandment

"Remember the Sabbath day, to keep it holy. Six days you shall labor and do all your work."

This Fourth Commandment quickly provokes in peoples' minds several questions, for example:

1. How important is this particular commandment?

Is it really to be considered as seriously as, let us say, the Sixth Commandment, "You shall not kill"? The answer: the Fourth Commandment belongs to the first table of the law: man's duties to God, and surely these are no less important than man's duties to his neighbor. Indeed, it should be strongly affirmed that man's relation to God is fundamental; so its violation is more crucial than a violation of any human relationship. Consequently, the worst evils are those of having other gods, worshiping graven images, taking God's name in vain, and failing to remember (or "observe," the word used in Deuteronomy 5) the Sabbath day.

These commandments appear first in the Decalogue. Thus observance is of urgent importance; for to break the Sabbath is an offense against God and more serious than any against man. Its importance is underscored by the fact that Israel's failure to keep the Sabbath was a capital offense:

> *"And the LORD said to Moses....You shall keep the Sabbath, because it is holy for you; every one who profanes it shall be put to death."* (Exodus 31:12, 14)

2. Doesn't the New Testament, however, minimize and perhaps even abolish Sabbath-keeping as a law?

The answer: first, the New Testament could not abolish one of the Ten Commandments anymore than some latter-day physicist could abolish the ancient law of gravity. The Decalogue does not contain man's changeable laws but the Divine order of the universe. Second, the New Testament does not abolish or abrogate the Old, but "fulfills" it. Jesus says:

> *"Think not that I have come to abolish the law and the prophets; I have come not to abolish the law and the prophets; I have come not to abolish them but to fulfill them. For truly, I say to you, till heaven and earth pass away, not an iota, not a dot, will pass from the law until all is accomplished."* (Matthew 5:17-18)

3. Do not Christians generally pay no heed to the Sabbath law, since the Sabbath was the seventh day of the week and the Christian observance centers upon Sunday, the first day of the week?

This is a question that not only the Jewish people ask of the Christians but also some Christians ask of fellow Christians. For example, the Seventh Day Adventists and Seventh Day Baptists follow the practice of "keeping" Saturday as the Sabbath and feel quite sincerely that most Christian churches break the Fourth Commandment through "Sunday observance."

The answer: no one can or would want to deny that the Sabbath in the Old Testament and much of the New Testament was the seventh day of the week, our Saturday. However, something happened in the New Testament of such magnitude that Christians soon began using the first day of the week for the usual Sabbath activities. This great event was the resurrection of Jesus Christ on the first day of the week. This was truly the LORD's Day—the day of victory over sin and death. So it was not long until that Day—the LORD's Day of triumph—became the Christian Sabbath. For example, in Acts we read: "*On the first day of the week...Paul talked with them*" (20:7); in 1 Corinthians Paul writes, "*On the first day of every week, each of you is to put something aside*" (16:2); in the Book of Revelation John says, "*I was in the Spirit on the LORD's Day*" (1:10).

So the change occurred, the Resurrection being the moving force. The Westminster Confession of Faith puts it this way: "...in His word, by a positive, moral and perpetual commandment, binding all men in all ages, He hath particularly appointed one day in seven for a Sabbath, to be kept holy unto him: which, from the beginning of the world to the resurrection of Christ was the last day of the week; and from the resurrection of Christ was changed into the first day of the week, which in Scripture is called the LORD's Day, and is to be continued to the end of the world as the Christian Sabbath" (Article XXI, 7-8).

Even in the Old Testament, the Fourth Commandment does not prescribe that the *last* day of the week be observed as the Sabbath. The commandment really is: six days of labor and one day of rest each week, "*Six days you shall labor, and do all your work; but the seventh day is a Sabbath*" (Exodus 20:9-10). The seventh day is to be an interlude; therefore, its designation as "last" day or "first" day—or any other particular shift from "last" day to "first" day—does not alter the Old Testament commandment. Indeed, here already is an illustration of the New Testament confirming and fulfilling the Old; a day to be kept holy to the LORD is made not the last event of the week but the first.

Let us move on from a discussion of the "particular day," and from other preliminary questions raised, to the all-important matter now before us, namely: *what is involved in a proper observance of the Sabbath?* To find an answer let us look first at the Old Testament teaching, second at the fulfillment of this teaching in Jesus Christ and, finally, at the testimony of the early church in the New Testament letters. In the Old Testament the Sabbath is *a day to be kept holy*: a "holy day." "Remember ('observe,' Deuteronomy 5) the Sabbath day, to keep it holy...the seventh day is a Sabbath to the LORD your God....the LORD blessed the Sabbath day and hallowed it" (Exodus 20:8, 10, 11). The Sabbath is therefore a day, first of all, honoring God; a day of recollection and observance of His mighty works.

The first of these divine acts to be remembered is that of *creation*: "In six days the LORD made heaven and earth, the sea and all that in them is, and rested the seventh day; therefore, the LORD blessed the Sabbath day and hallowed it" (Exodus 20:10,11). The Sabbath is a "rest day" (this we shall discuss more fully later), but one which brings to mind all the wonders of the six days of creation preceding it. The creation was no trivial matter or some effortless diversion of the Divine. It was work, hard work for God Almighty, and the Sabbath marked its glorious completion. Every Sabbath therefore should recall *God's marvelous self-giving in the work of creation.*

The second divine act to be remembered is that of *deliverance*: "You shall remember that you were a servant in the land of Egypt, and the LORD your God brought you out thence with a mighty hand and an outstretched arm; therefore the LORD your God commanded you to keep the Sabbath day" (Deuteronomy 5:15). The deliverance of Israel from bondage in Egypt by the mighty works of God is to be remembered on every Sabbath. This was not Israel's action, but the LORD's, and the Sabbath day is to call to mind God's complete salvation. The people were utterly lost until God reached out His powerful hand to save. Because of the creation of all things and the redemption from Egypt, the mighty acts of God are to be remembered on the Sabbath.

The Sabbath is, first of all, *a time for worship*. Since the Sabbath is to be kept holy through remembrance, what better way to remember than gathering for worship? By doing so, His mighty deeds can be rehearsed by singing. Gratitude, therefore, can be expressed, and dedication to His service may be offered.

The Sabbath then is a wonderful gift and opportunity to worship God. On this special day, people can turn aside from their usual routine of life, the affairs of man, and in holy convocation meditate upon God in His marvels of creation and salvation. In worshiping not only is God glorified but also people fulfill their highest goal and find their purest joy. In this there is rest for the soul; man is doing what he most deeply needs and longs for: he is worshiping the Eternal. Immediately this leads to the recognition of the Sabbath as a *day of rest*. True worship is rest to the soul, but in the Old Testament there is much stress on rest for the body also.

The Sabbath is not only a day to honor God through worship—and so find rest and renewal of soul—it is also a day to honor God by not working, thus finding rest and renewal of both mind and body. On the Sabbath one recalls God's mighty works, and also recalls that "on it God rested from all His work which He had done" (Genesis 2:3). To keep the Sabbath holy is therefore not only to meditate on the deeds of the Almighty, it is to follow His example and rest from labor. God worked six days and rested; so it must be with all of God's creatures:

> *"Six days you shall labor and do all your work; but the seventh day is a Sabbath to the LORD your God; in it you shall not do any work...for in six days the LORD made heaven and earth, the sea, and all that is in them, and rested the seventh day."*
>
> (Exodus 20:9-11)

The Sabbath, obviously, is a wonderful and merciful provision for man from his labor. He may, and must, work six days. But in those six days all work for the week must be completed (even as God completed all of His), and on the seventh he may—and must—rest (as God did) from all work. The commandment to work and to rest is equally binding—and equally liberating!

On this point, we see once again how God's commandments are life-giving. Not going to the right hand or to the left is to know true happiness. Labor is done better when there is a time of rest to anticipate; and rest is all the more enjoyed when "all your work" is finished. Such alternating of labor and rest brings both rich and full living.

Also, labor beyond six days is simply not rewarding. Actually, it is not more productive no matter what people may say. The story of the manna, the "bread from heaven," in Exodus 16, illustrates the futility of such work. The Israelites worked six days gathering the manna, laboring for their "daily bread," and when some went out to gather again on the seventh day there was none to be found. Their Sabbath labor was futile and wrong, for God actually had provided enough on the sixth day so that the Sabbath literally could be "a day of solemn rest, a holy Sabbath to the LORD" (verse 23). God gives bread for seven days in six days: how foolish, how wrong of man to try gaining more through work on the seventh!

To work on the seventh day is both to gain nothing and, of even more consequence, to lose greatly: the rich experience of worship plus rest for the body, mind, and soul.

It becomes apparent indeed, that proper Sabbath observance is quite essential to human life. Disobedience to the Fourth Commandment is not only a breach of divine law but also destructive to man's own well-being and nature. It is in appreciation of this fact that we can understand the fearful Old Testament penalty of death for working on the Sabbath:

> *"Six days shall work be done, but on the seventh day you shall have a holy Sabbath of solemn rest to the LORD; whoever does any work on it shall be put to death."* (Exodus 35:2)

Destruction to man's body, mind, and soul is the result of failure to keep the Sabbath. This death, gradual but relentless, is through his own foolishness and sin because the law of God and His very own nature are one and the same. Man cannot break the Sabbath and live. If he does not worship and rest, so reads the Word of God and the law of man's being, he shall surely die.

Is it not absurd that people so often go right ahead with this suicide? Although Almighty God rested on the seventh day, they do not feel it necessary for themselves and continue their labors. A man works five or six days at his business, and then feels he must spend the rest of the time working around the house, doing odd jobs of various kinds. There is no time for worship or rest; so he proceeds to kill himself: spiritually, mentally, and physically.

"Six days you shall labor, and do *all* your work"—*not some*, and leave a part, or another kind, of work for the Sabbath. Such work benefits nothing: it is slavery and slavery is death. Such work prevents all the heights of worship and renewal that the Sabbath may bring.

But what about the woman? "A man works till setting sun; a woman's work is never done," so the old saying goes. Man may labor for bread six days and so provide for the seventh. But people do eat seven days a week, and there is work connected with any meal. Does not the Fourth Commandment apply to the woman also, or is she doomed because she must break it so her family will not starve? The story in Exodus 16—already referred to—is illuminating in this regard: Moses said to his people, "Tomorrow is a day of solemn rest, a holy Sabbath to the LORD; bake what you will bake and boil what you will boil, and all that is left over lay by to be kept till morning" (verse 23).

In other words, the day before the Sabbath should be a day of preparation, so that as much work as possible be avoided on the "day of solemn rest." The work of boiling, baking and many other chores can be handled the day before, if one has the desire. When there is a will, there is quite often a way to do it. Surely the woman needs the worship and rest of the Sabbath as much as, if not sometimes more than, the rest of the family!

Sabbath-keeping can become an exciting adventure for individuals and families. When work is really limited to six days, and preparation is made for a full experience of worship and rest on the seventh, everyone benefits. Preparation for worship would include Bible reading, prayer, study of the Sunday School lesson, self-examination, even fasting at times. Preparation for rest would mean getting many jobs done during the week that would otherwise be left to do on the Sabbath and thinking through, ahead of time, what refreshing possibilities for body and mind the Sabbath can offer. With such and many other possibilities, one cannot help rejoicing in the blessedness of God's great gift: the Sabbath day! Some people, of course, must work on the Sabbath. Civilization in all its complexity will not permit all to cease from labor because there are works of necessity and mercy that must be done seven days of every week. What then can be said about the Fourth Commandment and Sabbath-workers? Two things: first, the Sabbath worker must be sure that his or her labor is truly necessary. Second, if it is a necessary work, then that person must be all the more determined to have another day of the week for a time of worship and rest.

As mentioned earlier, the main concern of the Fourth Commandment is that there be six days of labor and one of rest—for body, mind, and soul. The specific day is therefore not as important as the proper observance. It is, however, doubly hard for the Sabbath worker to observe another day, but the way will be provided through God's help, and the person's own ingenuity. His or her Sabbath can be just as rich and full, perhaps even more joyous than that of others, because that person has had to overcome much to achieve it.

In the New Testament teaching and example of Jesus, two things are to be noted: first, the Sabbath is viewed not only as an opportunity for the worship of God but also as *a day for the service of man*, and second: Jesus makes it transparently clear that *"the Sabbath was made for man, not man for the Sabbath"* (Mark 2:27).

The first of these points needs little elaboration, because the example of Jesus is evident everywhere. The Sabbath was, for Him, filled with "doing good" for many people. The first chapter of Mark (verses 21-34) contains a record of Jesus' activities on a certain Sabbath—probably illustrative of His usual practice.

First: He went into the synagogue and taught. Synagogue attendance, worship, teaching, etc., were the beginning of the Sabbath for the Master.

Second: He went to the home of Simon Peter and cured Simon's mother-in-law of a fever. Upon rising she served Him and the other disciples.

Third: when it was sundown, He healed many who were sick and cast out a number of demons.

The Sabbath contained *worship* in the synagogue, *rest* and *relaxation* in Peter's home—probably for the whole afternoon—and *service to people* in the morning, noon and night; the greatest measure being given at the end of the day. Worship, rest, deeds of mercy and kindness: a beautiful composite picture of a Sabbath day in the life of Jesus our Lord!

Jesus' example, then, is a welcome addition to the Old Testament picture of the Sabbath. Worship of God is basic, but worship, to be at its best, should overflow to the service of others. Love of God is inseparable from love of neighbors. To be drawn closer to God through worship is to be brought closer to all of God's creatures; to sense God's presence is to sense our fellowman's deepest needs. Therefore, worship that overflows immediately into the service to others is worship brought to its true culmination.

How seldom this process is actually realized! Many an individual worships on a Sabbath morning, rests of a Sabbath afternoon, but never thinks of how he may also devote the day to the service of others. There may be: a friend in need who could be visited or written to, a person in trouble who has no one to turn to, someone sick who needs solace and strength, or somebody lacking faith who requires help to find their way. Such opportunities for mercy and kindness are at hand every day of course, but truly on the Sabbath they may be given even more prayerful and devoted attention. Strength and wisdom to meet these challenges are also all the more present on the day of worship and rest; for with an uplifted soul and renewal of mind and body, one may better and more joyously minister to the necessities of others. The Sabbath is ideally a day for the service of one's fellowman.

The second thing Jesus underscored was that "the Sabbath was made for man, and not man for the Sabbath." This strong statement was made necessary by the unfortunate attitude of the Pharisees regarding the Sabbath. The Pharisees, rather than rejoicing in the opportunities for worship and rest which the Old Testament law made possible, felt constrained to pronounce judgment upon the nature of 'work.' Rather than enumerating the wonder of God's creation and redemption, and so helping people to a richer worship experience, and then suggesting the varied ways people and families might find rest and recreation on the Sabbath, they spent their time and energy ruling on 'work.' The result: the day of rest and gladness soon became a day of burdens and fear. With their hundreds of definitions of what work consisted of plus the fearful warnings that to do any of these things was to break the law of God, the Sabbath became a tyranny over man, restricting and enslaving. It was no longer a day for rejoicing.

So it was Jesus who broke the chains of bondage with His proclamation that "the Sabbath was made for man, not man for the Sabbath." The Sabbath is to allow man rest of soul, rest of body, and a freedom to love God and his neighbor. The Sabbath is servant, therefore, of even the most important living human being. For the Sabbath to become a tyrannical burden is to pervert one of the most wonderful gifts God ever gave to His creation!

By a strange twist of Christian history, the Pharisaism of the New Testament—with its countless taboos and activities classified as work—has at times shifted to taboos regarding various forms of rest and recreation. This latter day Pharisaism, sometimes called Puritanism, instead of ruling out certain activities because they contain work, has ruled out certain activities because they contain pleasure! The Pharisees of the New Testament decided that if a commandment prohibits work on the Sabbath, they ought to make it clear just what work is.

The Puritans of church history decided that if a commandment declared that the Sabbath is to be kept holy, they ought to make it clear what forms of rest were unholy. In other words, Puritanical concern about the Sabbath and rest was *not* about pleasurable activities considered by them to be wrong *every* day of the week (gambling, drinking, dancing, card playing, etc.), and therefore taboo on weekdays as well as the Sabbath. Their concern, in regard to the Sabbath, rather, was about pleasurable activities considered to be *right* during the week but on the Sabbath—being a holy day—these same activities were considered wrong regardless *of how much they might help man to rest*. These activities were not wrong during the week when a man ought to be working, but they were wrong on Sunday when a man ought to be resting! Such peculiar and perverse distinctions of the Puritans, eating away at the joy of the Sabbath, were all done in the name of "Sabbath-keeping." Actually, even more than the Pharisees who over-burdened the Sabbath with their fine distinctions about work, the Puritans overwhelmed and almost destroyed the Sabbath with their hard-line distinctions of pleasure.

Surely "to keep the Sabbath holy" is to keep it as God intended: a day of abounding *worship, rest, and service.* To try removing elements of rest, in the name of holiness, is tragically evil. Any pleasurable activity, innocent in itself, that may afford rest to body and mind should be gladly entered into. To abstain, actually, is failing to keep the Sabbath. Worship and service are not enough: there ought also to be genuine rest. If the restful activity is legitimate during the week, it is even more legitimate on the Sabbath—and by enjoying it to the fullest on the Sabbath a person is truly helping to keep the Sabbath holy.

This Puritanical perversion has almost destroyed the Sabbath for countless people, for the word "Sabbath" has come to signify, "Thou shall not enjoy thyself on this day." Rather than being the day of highest joy through worship of God, happy rest and recreation, and glad service to others, it has seemed like a sober, repressive strait-jacket. Therefore the Fourth Commandment has for numbers of people become despised and detested; and one of God's most wondrous gifts to mankind, the Sabbath day, has been both destroyed and lost.

The words of Jesus, "the Sabbath was made for man, and not man for the Sabbath," are, however, a cry of liberation to those over-burdened by Pharisaical and Puritanical distinctions about both work and rest. Even as His Spirit cut through the perversities of the New Testament world, it can also break through the perversities of any day, including our own, and lead us forward into a new and even richer appreciation of the holy Sabbath.

Finally, in the New Testament letters, only two direct references to the Sabbath are made: the first of these references is in Hebrews 4:9 where the writer says: "So then, there remains a Sabbath rest for the people of God." The reference here is to the event when labor is done and rest is at last achieved. "Sabbath" and "rest" are therefore terms for the gift of God, made to those who remain obedient to the end.

More relevant to our consideration so far is the second reference found in Colossians 2:16-18: "Let no one pass judgment on you in questions of food and drink or with regard to a festival or a new moon or a Sabbath. These are only a shadow of what is to come; but the substance belongs to Christ. Let no one disqualify you."

Paul's great concern is that the Christian church never become a center for judgment and counter-judgment on such matters as eating, drinking, and Sabbath-keeping. He urges that no one feel disqualified if others decide if he or she is not doing these things the "right" way.

The New Testament ends with what is certainly a good word. It is a warning against the Pharisees of every age, and a recognition that the substance, the real truth, always belongs to Christ. Staying close to Him, His teaching, and His example is to find increasingly the way to abundant living, and to see in the Sabbath one of God's richest gifts to His creation.

"Remember the Sabbath day, to keep it holy."

This commandment, as all others, is a roadway to life. Walk on it and worship truly, rest wisely, serve gladly—then your walk shall be upon the high places of the earth!

Notes and Meditation:

The Fifth Commandment

"Honor your father and your mother."

Let us now look at the Fifth Commandment in the context of the total relationship between parents and children. In order to do so, we will begin by noting the significant words of Ephesians 6:1-4:

> *"Children, obey your parents in the Lord, for this is right. 'Honor your father and mother' (this is the first commandment with a promise) 'that it may be well with you and that you may live long on the earth.' Fathers, do not provoke your children to anger, but bring them up in the discipline and instruction of the Lord."*

"Children, obey your parents in the Lord" is speaking of a Christian home in which it is assumed that the parents are Christian; and being Christian themselves are "in the Lord." In other words, the parents have a higher authority than themselves to whom they are obedient—Jesus Christ the Lord—and, even as they stand under this higher authority, so their children are under them. The parents, then, are not the final law; but they must do all things unto God—humbly seeking His will. Therefore, they cannot be tyrants or lords over their children. Children must obey because they are not yet of age to exercise full responsibility of decision; but in

obeying, if their parents are truly Christian, they are really giving obedience to Christ.

Truly it is a fearful thing to be a Christian parent or parents, because our children must be taught complete obedience to our words and commands. Therefore, we must be equally concerned that our words and commands come from the Lord. This complete obedience is actually necessary for the good of the child. An illuminating story is told of a little girl whose day was a tale of one misbehavior after another, with interspersed scolding by her mother. She finally set herself firmly in an armchair with the words, 'I wish father would come home and *make* me behave!' "

A child wants to obey, wants laws that are not to be broken, hungers for a solid moral universe and a stable home. Such laws must not be just the parents' own pet ideas, whims, expressions of irritation, selfishness, and laws and commands that do not concern the child's welfare, but the parents' own. This means that parents have the responsibility of making those laws clear, being sure the commands come from God, and are always in the best interests of the child.

Parents, therefore, have the great responsibility—belonging to no one else in quite the same way—of rightly expecting obedience from their children; and unless they humbly seek God's guidance to express His truth, love, and wisdom, they are bound to fail. They will become tyrants breaking their children's will through selfish commands or—equally bad—will not be true parents at all, allowing their children to do as they please; thus living in a state of emptiness and rebellion.

Your children must obey you because you represent God to them, and they really do want to obey. Are you satisfying their desire by being consistent and steadfast in your laws; laws that are not your own ideas alone but which are an expression of God's will and purpose as you discover them through the Scriptures, prayers, and, most of all the example of Jesus Christ? How desperately parents need to be "in the Lord"—with all the expression implies to exercise their fearful and also wonderful responsibility. "Children, obey your parents in the Lord, for this is right."

"Fathers, do not provoke your children to anger, but bring them up in the discipline and instruction of the Lord." Fathers are addressed here not to exclude mothers but, because of being the head of the house, it is assumed that whatever pattern they lay down will be shared by their wives. If the father is not alive, or is away very much, the responsibility passes to the mother. "Fathers and mothers, provoke not your children to anger." How are parents to fulfill this specific charge?

First, in the way already mentioned: namely, by providing a moral atmosphere where the children may live—a world in which they sense that, although they must obey their parents, the parents are also under a higher authority themselves. Parents who are "not their own" but belong to God—whose commands therefore are of God and not human only—will not provoke their children to anger. A child may be fitful and rebellious at times, but as he or she comes to sense more and more that they also are under orders, the child will be ready and willing to obey.

Second, by seeking daily to bring up their children in the discipline and instruction of the Lord. The King James Version says: to bring up your children "in the nurture and admonition of the Lord." Fathers, mothers too, would you like to rear your children without provoking any wrath or anger? If so, then bring them up in the nurture, admonition, discipline, and instruction of the Lord.

Indeed, this is a serious vow. If parents are to live up to it, they must strive, in every way possible with God's help, to bring the children up in the knowledge of God, an understanding of the Bible, a vital faith in Jesus Christ, a love for the church, a yearning to do God's will, and a concern for other people's welfare and salvation. Have we, as parents, tried to live up to this, or have we provoked our children to anger by causing them to miss the true wonder of Christian living?

A child has the right to: know God, learn to pray, and love God's Kingdom; if his parents fail him, he has been hurt forever. Will your child be angry—and rightly so—because you cheated him out of his spiritual rights? "My father failed me: he sent me to Sunday School but seldom came himself, he never gathered us for prayer in our home, and he made Sunday just like any other day—I was cheated." Will your son or your daughter say those words in anger someday? Or will it be too late for that child, already stripped by you of a religious heritage, to be able to say anything at all?

Some children are saved in spite of their parents; some find the way to the Kingdom through God's grace, though parents have never lived up to their vows. However, that does not release parents from having been very neglectful. If you have been such parents, it is high time you pray to God for forgiveness and mercy—and thank Him that He saved those you would have lost—begging Him humbly to receive you into His Kingdom. "Fathers do not provoke your children to anger, but bring them up in the discipline and instruction of the Lord."

Third, "Honor your father and mother." We come now to the third charge (actually the second in the sequence of Ephesians 6:1-4) and a consideration of the Fifth Commandment in the Decalogue.

The first two charges have been addressed to children and parents: children in the home who must obey parents "in the Lord" and parents in the home who must bring up their children "in the Lord." The third is concerned more specifically about the relation of adults: children who have reached maturity, who may have even left home to establish their own homes, and their parents. These grown children do not owe any obedience; rather they have moved to a higher level, namely of honoring the parents.

Perhaps it is surprising to some that "Honor your father and your mother" is elevated to such an important commandment. It is according to the usual numbering system the Fifth Commandment, after the first four that are concerned about God: no other Gods, no graven images, no taking God's name in vain, no working on God's day; and is prior to all the commandments having to do with one's fellowman—no killing, no adultery, no stealing, and so on.

Is to dishonor parents an even worse evil than killing, stealing, or lying? The answer: note that the Old Testament makes clear different kinds of dishonor to parents. The famous commandment reads:

"Honor your father and your mother, that your days may be long in the land which the LORD your God gives you."

Now look across at Exodus 21:15 and 17 which reads:

"Whoever strikes his father or his mother shall be put to death....Whoever curses his father or his mother shall be put to death."

Regardless of the provocation, for one to strike or curse his father or mother is to forfeit one's life: to be put to death. Killing, on the other hand, as the Old Testament shows, is not always a capital offense; it depends on the provocation—this we shall note later in our discussion of the Sixth Commandment—but dishonoring, in the sense of striking or cursing a parent, very definitely merits the death of the offender. So, as we see, the Fifth Commandment, in importance, precedes the Sixth and the commands of the Decalogue that follow.

"But," someone may press, "Isn't that just Old Testament teaching? Surely the New Testament would never think of dishonor to a parent as meriting death." The answer to that question is found when Jesus quotes the Fifth Commandment and, likewise without criticism, quotes the law about the gravity of this offense:

> *"For God commanded, 'Honor your father and your mother,' and 'He who speaks evil of father or mother, let him surely die.'"*
>
> (Matthew 15:4)

Why is this the case? The answer is doubtless that however good or bad parents may have been or are, they do in some sense represent God to their children. God is the heavenly Father without whom no life can be sustained. Also, without fathers and mothers watching over their newborn infants—providing for, feeding, carrying them about—no one's life could have been sustained. Parents do represent God, even though many fail almost completely to rear their children in the nurture and admonition of the LORD.

Another fact, both important and very obvious, is that none of us would exist in the first place without our parents. If your father had not married your mother, there would not have been a "you" in the world. But they did marry, and God blessed their marriage by sending a child, perhaps children. With your parents sharing in God's wondrous act of creation, they deserve honor therefore as those by whom God created you. Genesis 1 and 2 describe God's marvelous act of creation of heaven and earth; Genesis 4 continues with the act of creation of a child:

> *"Now Adam knew Eve his wife, and she conceived and bore Cain, saying, 'I have gotten a man with the help of the LORD.'"*

One can detect Eve's excitement, wonder, and thrill in those words—to think that God would continue his creation through the miracle of childbirth! And ever since, no one has been born into this world without human parents; parents who by coming together and bringing forth a child, share in God's ongoing creation.

Parents, by virtue of their place in continuing creation and by sustaining our lives when we were utterly dependent—and for many other reasons—deserve a place of honor and respect as long as we are alive. To honor them, whatever their character may be, is to honor God who through them brought us into the world.

This is why the Fifth Commandment belongs in the first half of the Decalogue: the commandments relating to God, because parents are God's instruments of both our creation and preservation. Therefore, let us never get to the place where such honor ceases—even if we claim religious motivation. In this regard, note the incident in Matthew 15:1-9 about Jesus' severe indictment of those, who, in making a religious vow, think they no longer have any responsibility to their parents.

Jesus is not in agreement with the scribes and Pharisees: they are concerned because He does not "uphold" the "tradition of the elders"—a collection of practices that have grown up alongside the Old Testament, such as the ritual washing of hands before eating. Jesus does not answer their criticism directly; but counters by asking why, for the sake of the tradition, they transgress the commandment of God. He illustrates in relation to the Fifth Commandment, "Honor your father and mother," by questioning one of their traditions; namely, that it is quite proper to give God what would otherwise have been given to one's parent or parents.

In other words, if you have set aside a certain amount of money to help your father and mother in their old age and they are counting on it, but instead you give it to God, then according to tradition, you are discharged from your obligation to help them: put God first, and as long as you do that, you can forget all filial responsibility.

The Pharisees loved that kind of tradition because it meant more money in their pockets, and, since they really had no care for any human need, they closed their eyes to the fact that they themselves, who talked so loudly about the law, were transgressing it utterly as well as teaching others to do the same.

Truly God must be first, but Jesus insists that this priority does not mean that one is excused from all other obligations, especially those toward one's own parents. This neglect, approved by the Pharisees, is truly worse than hitting, or cursing, or speaking evil. Such parents are forgotten and alone, and their children, for all their pretense of religious devotion, stand under the judgment of Almighty God. If speaking against parents merits death, what then of neglect? As we have seen, the answer is very obvious indeed.

It must be mentioned here that there are some verses in the New Testament where Jesus *seems* to counsel neglect of parents. The most familiar incident probably is when He says to a certain man, "Follow me," and the man replies, "Lord, let me first go and bury my father." Jesus then answered, "Leave the dead to bury their own dead; but as for you, go and proclaim the kingdom of God" (Luke 9:59-60).

Does it not seem strange, in view of Jesus' great stress on honoring parents, that He should tell a man not even to bury his father, but go and proclaim the kingdom of God? Does He perhaps sound like the Pharisees who, according to their tradition, would free a man from filial responsibility if he put God first? It may sound the same, but actually there is a world of difference.

Notice carefully: this man was putting his father before God, but God must always be first. God is the absolute priority, but this man was saying, "Let me *first* go and bury my father"—which was the wrong priority. If he had placed God first, His kingdom and its righteousness, then he could have attended better to the burial of his father. Indeed, with God first in his life, the burial would have been a wonderful act of faith and love with the son rendering true honor.

Note: it is no true honor to parents to place them first, before God, because by dishonoring God you actually dishonor them. Sometimes a person hears a statement as, "I'm sorry that I can't attend church, or serve in a church program, because I have to care for my parents," or, "I'm sorry for not giving to the church but all I have goes for them." Wait, wait a moment: unless God is first in time, talents, and money—it is dishonor from beginning to end.

Finally, this needs to be said: "Honor to parents" is not "obedience." A child owes obedience, but an adult owes honor. Indeed sometimes disobedience, when a person has come to maturity, is necessary—if parents are not willing for the transition from obedience to honor to take place. At times, only through disobedience, when a person places God before his parents and his parents' wishes, is true honor shown.

You may remember the story of Garth, the young knight of the Round Table in Arthurian legend, whose mother had looked forward to Gareth's growing up and to the day when he would be a gentleman, a sportsman on the chase, hunting deer, and so forth? At last Gareth stood before his mother, and felt constrained to say:

"Man I am grown, a man's work must I do,
Follow the deer? Follow the Christ, the King,
Live pure, speak true, right wrong. Follow the King—
Else, wherefore born?"[7]

Disobedient to a parent out of a higher loyalty to God, he showed true honor and thereby fulfilled the Fifth Commandment through and through.

God truly honors those who honor Him, and in doing so honor their parents. Even if one's parents should no longer be alive, honor is still possible by always mentioning their names with respect, giving thanks to God in prayer for them, visiting their place of burial with loving concern, and always being humbly aware that God brought them together and through them brought you into the world.

If they are quite elderly, express your appreciation while still possible, see what need they have that you may meet, think of their comfort before you own, and pray for them day and night; this is showing true honor. If one or both is not a Christian, there can be no higher way of honoring them than to believe that they will still be, and to do all you can to direct them to His heavenly kingdom.

"Honor your father and your mother." By doing this you will know length of days and blessings forever.

Notes and Meditation:

The Sixth Commandment

"You shall not kill."

Coming to the Sixth Commandment, we move quite clearly to the commandments that deal with man's relation to others: "You shall not kill; you shall not commit adultery, you shall not steal, you shall not bear false witness, and you shall not covet." "You shall not kill" reads the Sixth Commandment.

Since we believe this to be the very law of God, we must be greatly concerned about obeying it. Unquestionably, as with other commandments, obedience is not only due because it is a divine command, but also because to obey is to live in this world in the happiest way possible.

At first glance the meaning of the Sixth Commandment may seem quite obvious and simple. It says not to kill, so all killing is wrong—anything, any person, at any time. But is that what the Commandment really means in the context of the Old Testament?

For example, there are some people who call themselves "*vegetarians*." They eat no meat. Some vegetarians say they abstain from meat because of the Sixth Commandment. "You shall not kill" means, they argue, that no life is to be destroyed, animal or human. Are those "vegetarians" right? Does the Sixth Commandment prohibit killing of animals? Not at all, because throughout the Bible's Old and New Testaments, the killing of animals is never considered wrong: whether it be for food or sacrifice to God. Some animals mentioned in the Old Testament are not to be eaten, but all may be killed; and everywhere we read of the slaying of animals, so commanded by God, for sacrifice. "You shall not kill" in the Bible does not include animals.

Some people also argue that the Sixth Commandment prohibits *capital punishment*. "You shall not kill" may not include animals; but man—they ask—doesn't it include all human beings? If that were so, then of course, regardless of whatever crime a person may have committed, that person should never be put to death.

Some time ago, the Illinois House of Representative voted for a six year moratorium on the death sentence. Regardless of the crime: treason, murder, kidnapping—all of which at the time were subject to capital punishment, if this bill had also passed the Senate and the governor had signed, there would have been no capital punishment in Illinois for at least six years.[8] Why such a moratorium?

According to the press releases: some argued that capital punishment had proved no deterrent to crime and therefore was no longer of value, and others argued that it cost the state and defendants too much to go through all the court appeals after a judgment of death had been sentenced. But no one—it was of real significance to note—argued against capital punishment on the basis of the Sixth Commandment or the Bible as a whole. Surely this restraint was wise, because the Bible clearly affirms capital punishment.

Someone might even complete the Sixth Commandment this way: "You shall not kill, and if you do you will be killed in return." Long before the Ten Commandments were given (Exodus 20), God had said to Noah (Genesis 9): "Whoever sheds the blood of man, by man shall his blood be shed." In addition to the Ten

Commandments, many other commandments provide for the death penalty if broken. A person can turn to Exodus 21—immediately following the Decalogue—to read of capital punishment for many additional offenses.

It is argued, however, that capital punishment is wrong because of the New Testament teaching about love. The passage most often cited is Matthew 5:38 and following:

"You have heard that it was said, 'An eye for an eye and a tooth for a tooth.' But I say to you, 'Do not resist one who is evil. But if anyone strikes you on the right cheek, turn to him the other also....love your enemies and pray for those who persecute you.'"

Plainly this passage has nothing to do with capital punishment. It stands in strong opposition to vengeful reprisals, and suggests a positive method of dealing with one's enemies. The enemy is always to be loved, never hated. But again, these words of Jesus are not concerned with capital punishment; they are dealing with human relations, the kind that exists wherever the Kingdom of God is present.

Indeed, the death penalty for certain crimes is assumed throughout the New Testament. Recall Jesus' quoting, without criticism, the Old Testament law, "He who speaks evil of father or mother, let him surely die" (Matthew 15:4). Jesus doubtless meant, in addition, that dishonor to a parent is fatal to one's spirit. Recall that He does not add to that particular commandment, one of His "But I say to you...." He lets it stand with the death penalty. Capital punishment is the rule of the Bible for certain crimes against God and man. Love in the New Testament never rules out justice.

Some people argue that the Sixth Commandment prohibits *war* and the killing that is inevitably involved. Many people have raised the question, "Can a Christian go to war and kill without, at the same time, breaking the Sixth Commandment?" The answer is not an easy one, but it is way too simple to say, on a biblical basis, that all killing in wartime is wrong.

First look at the Old Testament. There is obviously no thought that war is forbidden by the Sixth Commandment. For example, Israel is told many times how to make war against her enemies, for example:

> *"When you draw near to a city to fight against it, offer terms of peace to it...but if it makes no peace with you....you shall besiege it; and when the LORD your God gives it into your hand you shall put all its males to the sword."*
> (Deuteronomy 20:10, 12, 13)

Obviously, not only was killing not wrong, but not killing heathen people practicing idol worship was wrong. Israel was the scourge in the hand of God to bring His justice to wicked peoples. Later, of course, Israel was destroyed herself, except for a remnant, because of her own evil ways. Those evil ways, however, did not include war.

In the New Testament, there is no basic change of that viewpoint. When, for example, soldiers ask John the Baptist what they should do to mend their ways, he does not tell them to stop fighting, but to "rob no one by violence or false accusation" (Luke 3:14). Jesus Himself says, "They that take the sword shall perish by the sword," and in another place, He uses a military illustration: "What king going to encounter another king in war, will not sit down first and take counsel whether he is able with ten thousand to meet him who comes against him with twenty thousand?" (Luke 14:31)

As seen throughout the New Testament, war with its accompanying killing is not in itself proclaimed to be wrong.

The answer to war is not always simple. Some "going to war" is no more than going forth to murder—and that certainly does break the Sixth Commandment. Other wars are justified when the God-given values of freedom of worship, speech, etc. are about to be destroyed. What we can never say is "My country, right or wrong," for we are a nation under God; and unless our country is fighting for a Godly principle, war cannot be justified. So the answer is not always a simple one, even though the final rule of action—that one may have to fight for what is right—is Biblical throughout.

War is a terrible business, but to say as some pacifists do, "I won't have anything to do with war," may be to surrender to evil: an evil that can destroy the most advanced and best of civilizations. Also, though nobody likes to kill, it may become necessary to do so to save countless others from being killed.

This has been far too brief considering the subject, but right now we cannot keep talking about war any longer. May we again stress the one point originally made, specifically: the Sixth Commandment does not in itself prohibit killing during war.

Actually the Sixth Commandment may best be interpreted as, "You shall not murder."[9] Three times now, we have noted that *the real point of the commandment is its steadfast opposition to all taking of life without due cause.* Animals may be killed to supply a sufficient food supply for men as well as for sacrifice to God; a man's life may be taken justly if he has committed an offense sufficiently warranting it; and finally, lives may be taken in wartime if the cause for which one is fighting is sufficiently worthy. The reason all these things involving killing are right is because they actually tend to the preservation of life. All other killing is actually murder, and murder is always wrong. "You shall not murder" is, then, the eternal command of Almighty God.

Right now we have much more important business before us than to discuss vegetarianism, capital punishment, and war. We must come to the far more profound meaning of the Sixth Commandment as the New Testament unfolds it.

Having come this far in our study of the Sixth Commandment, "You shall not kill," we may be inclined to think that, at last, we do not have to feel guilty! We may be saying to ourselves: "The first five commandments I know I've broken; I confess I've put other gods before Almighty God, I've worshiped graven images, I've taken God's name in vain, I've not always kept the Sabbath day holy, I've not done too well at times with honoring my father and my mother—all these commandments I've broken, and I need Divine forgiveness. But to my knowledge, I've never killed anyone, and surely I haven't murdered anybody. What a relief to talk about one commandment that I've indeed kept—and therefore don't need God's grace and God's forgiveness."

If these are our thoughts, it will be rather disconcerting while reading the New Testament to realize how much we fail to keep the Sixth Commandment; and how yes indeed we do need God's help.

This is important: the New Testament, in the words of Jesus, makes it unmistakably clear that killing is far more than an outward act of taking a person's life; it is also an inward act of anger or hatred that kills a person's own soul.

> *"You have heard that it was said to the men of old, 'You shall not kill; and whoever kills shall be liable to judgment.' But I say to you that everyone who is angry with his brother shall be liable to judgment; whoever insults his brother shall be liable to the council, and whoever says 'You fool!' shall be liable to the hell of fire."*
> (Sermon on the Mount, Matthew 5:21-22)

To be angry with one's brother, one's neighbor, or anyone is also to be liable to judgment in the eyes of God. Why? Because to be angry with someone is to wound not only his own body but his soul—and is not that self-wounding a mortal sin? "Do not fear those who kill the body but cannot kill the soul; rather fear him who can destroy both soul and body in hell" (Matthew 10:28).

Indeed, a murderous act, when someone destroys a person's body—for all its heinousness—is not as vicious or evil as the murderous action of anger or hatred that kills the soul. To take a life deserves a life in return; which means that when a soul is taken, a soul should be taken in return. It is to be worthy of not just physical death but, in the fearsome words of Jesus, to be worthy of the fires of hell.

Remember how the New Testament puts it in another place: "Anyone who hates his brother is a murderer, and you know that no murderer has eternal life" (1 John 3:15). Hatred is murder—someone does not have to go on to killing the other person's body, hatred itself *is* murder—it kills the soul. The result: no eternal life for the murderer. Rather, even as he who murders, he who hates is worthy of the fires of hell.

Let us look even more closely at anger, and note its fearful nature. First, we observe that anger often leads to physical murder. Recall the Old Testament story of Cain's murder of his brother Abel. What lay behind it? We read in Genesis 4:5: "So Cain was very angry, and his countenance fell." Shortly later he murdered his brother. Anger led to murder; without anger the murder would not have occurred. Therefore, when Jesus went behind the Sixth Commandment forbidding murder to forbid anger, He was striking at the intentions of the heart. Anger always contains a desire to kill. The desire, He is insisting, is just as wrong as the act itself. "You shall not kill" becomes, under Jesus, "You shall not be angry."

Secondly, anger is a fearful evil, not only because it often does lead to physical murder but also, as previously suggested, because it contains murder in its own nature. In other words, anger not only may lead to murder, it is murder; and whenever expressed, it kills life internally and all around externally.

Who of us therefore has not broken the Sixth Commandment? No, we may never have killed a person's body; but we know, to our sorrow and shame and guilt, that through anger and hate we have wounded some, perhaps many, peoples' souls even to death. Lord, have mercy on us all.

"But," someone may say, "This matter of anger, is it *always* wrong? Isn't there a time for anger, can't anger be a good thing?" The answer is "Yes," as long as it is God's kind of anger and not ours. Frequently the Bible, especially the Old Testament, speaks of the "anger of the LORD." This anger is always against one thing and one thing only, namely: the sin, the wickedness, the wrongdoing of mankind. For example:

"They forsook the LORD, and served the Baals and the Ashtaroth. So the anger of the LORD was kindled against... them." (Judges 2:13-14)

Of Jesus it is said in the New Testament, that He was also angered at wickedness:

"And He said to them, 'Is it lawful on the Sabbath to do good or to do harm, to save life or to kill?' But they were silent. And He looked around them with anger, grieved at their hardness of heart."
(Mark 3:4-5)

Anger against sin, yes, even fierce, hot anger, is always right; in fact is necessary. To watch evil dispassionately, to gaze upon it without feeling, is inhuman and un-Christian. To burn vigorously against evil is to be angry with the anger of heaven—and to be Christian: Christ-like. We need more angry people in the world in this sense: angry at every abuse of justice, angry at evil wherever it rears its ugly head; in racial discrimination, political scandal, economic exploitation, and temptations to immorality. Many of the finest advances in the human race have been accomplished through people angry enough at evil to strike it violently in the face and willing to suffer, even die, that the abuse might be annihilated.

This is all true but, unfortunately, most of the anger in the world is not this kind of righteous indignation. The world's anger is sinful. It is what the New Testament calls "the anger of man." Remember the statement in James 1:19 and 20:

"Let every man be quick to hear, slow to speak, slow to anger, for the anger of man does not work the righteousness of God."

This "anger of man" is Cain's kind of anger, springing from jealousy, envy or hurt pride. Abel seemed to be "getting ahead" in life: his offering from the flock was accepted by God, and Cain's offering from the soil, the fruit of the ground, was not. Cain was furious. The anger was unrighteous and loaded with murder. Indeed, Cain covered it up pretty well by giving a cordial-sounding invitation to his brother, "Let us go out into the field." But this invitation to fellowship accepted by Abel was filled with evil for: "when they were in the field, Cain rose up against his brother Abel, and killed him" (Genesis 4:8).

Thus the anger that roots in resentment, envy, jealousy, hurt pride, and competitiveness—who of us does not know these—is murder. When we see another "get ahead," we find all kinds of faults with him, imputing evil motives to his actions. Also, though outwardly and in his presence we may seem calm and collected and outgoing, inwardly we are filled with anger and are eager to destroy. We judge behind his back, we are critical of his methods and motives, and for what reason? Not because we are really angry at evil, which is God's kind of anger and right, but because we are trying to justify ourselves and cover-up our own sin. Frankly, we would like to see the person "dead and gone," not because there would be less evil around but that we might be "on top" again.

God have mercy! This kind of anger, whether expressed in some outward action of calling the person names such as "Raca" and "Fool" or—as is more often the case—cuddling it inwardly and allowing it to attack the other person in a roundabout but all the more vicious way, is murder. It not only thoroughly destroys the other person, but also makes oneself subject to the fires of Gehenna, which burn inwardly and outwardly both now and forever.

Is there any wonder that the New Testament counsels, again and again, against "the anger of man?" "But now put them all away: anger, wrath, malice, slander, and foul talk from your mouth" (Colossians 3:8). "In every place...men should pray, lifting holy hands without anger or quarreling" (1 Timothy 2:8). "The anger of man does not work the righteousness of God" (James 1:20).

What kind of a killer am I? What kind are you? How many murders are there in our record books lately? Have we been angry, *not at sin, but because of sin in ourselves*? If so, we have been killers also!

As husbands: have we been angry with our own wives, not really because of their faults however many or few they may have, but because we are selfish and do not really want to live up to our own responsibilities? If so, our anger is murder, and the fires of hell are inside us.

As parents: have we been angry with our children, not really because of their faults, but because we are selfish and do not want to be bothered enough: to show them the right way, talk to them as people, and to seek an understanding of their desires and needs? If so, our anger is murder, and fires of hell are burning inside again. In the workplace we may have been angry with our fellow workers: those above, below, or around us, not really because of their faults, but because of our own selfishness, pride and unconcern about them: their true needs, hopes, and ambitions? If so, our anger is murder, and the fires of hell burn yet again. How many murders are there? The answer is: we are all guilty.

Please, let us look for a moment at the cross of Calvary—a cross on which Somebody died. No, wait a moment, where Somebody was killed—killed by angry people. The cross is still there, because the killing is still going on. It goes on wherever there is anger, hate, malice, and wrath. The killing is not just of our fellowman, wives or husbands, children, associates, or friends. It is also the slaying of the heart of God. It is continually the crucifixion of the Lord of glory.

We are all killers, and deserve only the judgment of Almighty God. Yet because of His rich mercy and wonderful grace—love, compassion, forgiveness, and salvation still flow down from that very same cross, to anyone who cries out, "Lord, be merciful to me a sinner." As always, new life comes to those who yearn to live their days in the service of God and man.

"You shall not kill." Yes Lord, we reply. We will not any longer, if You are with us in strength, guidance, love and compassion, both now and always.

Notes and Meditation:

The Seventh Commandment

"You shall not commit adultery"

"So the LORD God caused a deep sleep to fall upon the man, and while he slept took one of his ribs and closed up its place with flesh; and the rib which the LORD God had taken from the man he made into a woman and brought her to the man. Then the man said, 'This at last is bone of my bones and flesh of my flesh; she shall be called Woman, because she was taken out of Man.' Therefore a man leaves his father and his mother and cleaves to his wife, and they become one flesh."

(Genesis 2:21-24)

Marriage, in its highest perspective as God ordained it to be, is a holy relationship in which a man and a woman become "one flesh." They are no more two; they have become one. No longer is the blood tie of a man to his father and mother the closest; rather he leaves them and after that forever "cleaves to his wife."

Man is not "one flesh" with his parents even though he was born to them; he is "one flesh" only with the wife God gives him. Woman, who was "taken from" man and therefore made for him, is "brought" by God to man. Marriage, then, is the holy fulfillment of the plan and purpose of God: to make two people one. This is how creation finds its climax: not in sun, moon, and stars; not in the wonder of life teeming in the seas, on the earth, or in the air, not even in the creation of man as man, *but* in the creation of man as male and female, husband and wife. The mystery, the miracle, the pinnacle of creation is: "They become one flesh."

It is against this background, of a high and holy understanding of the meaning of marriage, that the Seventh Commandment speaks with unmistakable brevity and force: "You shall not commit adultery." To commit adultery is an unthinkable and horrible act, for it means clearly: *the tearing asunder of the one flesh which God has united.* It is a type of murder—and that of the most vicious kind. Taking a weapon and cutting a person in half is a ghastly thing to contemplate. Adultery is the same: two who have become one are torn apart. God's highest act of creation is destroyed. This is why adultery is so thoroughly and utterly evil.

The penalty therefore, as the Old Testament declares it, cannot be anything except death. "If a man commits adultery with the wife of his neighbor, both the adulterer and the adulteress shall be put to death" (Leviticus. 20:10).

Adultery brings *death into the home* by striking a fatal blow to the delicate and wonderful relationship between husband and wife. It brings *death into man's relation with God* by its abominable sinfulness; what God has joined together man has put asunder. It brings *death to the individual,* adulterer and the adulteress, because each has killed his own flesh—and this is suicide: "He who commits adultery has no sense; he who does it destroys himself" (Proverbs 6:23).

Let us now come to a fuller consideration of the entire scope of the Seventh Commandment. If adultery is indeed such a great evil, both in what it does to a high and holy relationship as well as in the penalty it inevitably brings, we must be greatly concerned about knowing of what it is really composed.

Three things may be said: adultery, in its most obvious form, *may be committed by a man and a woman through a relationship which violates any marriage.*

An adulterer may himself be married and, if so, may commit adultery by any physical relationship outside his own marriage or, vice versa, the wife towards someone else. An adulterer may be unmarried himself and, if so, may commit adultery by entering into a physical relationship with a married woman, or again vice versa. In other words, the Seventh Commandment is concerned again with maintaining the sacredness of marriage: whoever, wed or unwed, violates this holy institution commits adultery.

The Old Testament story of David and Bathsheba (2 Samuel 11) illustrates in vivid and tragic fashion adultery *within* a marriage. David, though married, takes the beautiful Bathsheba (wife of Uriah) to himself. The result: Uriah is murdered by David to get him out-of-the-way, the child of this illicit union dies, and David is deeply disturbed. Therefore he confesses his great sin, and God spares his life—but not without David having to suffer and continuing to suffer all the result of his wrongdoing. This act of adultery was only a "momentary slip," but since it violated the highest and holiest relationship of man and wife, death was its tragic harvest.

Another story from the Old Testament, that of Joseph and Potiphar's wife (Genesis 39), illustrates an attempted case of adultery *outside* of marriage. Joseph, unmarried, was "handsome and good-looking," and while overseer of Potiphar's house was approached daily by Potiphar's wife. However, Joseph "would not listen to her, lie with her or be with her." His stalwart reply to the passionate woman:

"You are his [Potiphar's] wife, how then can I do this great wickedness, and sin against God?"

The result: through the thwarted woman's schemes, he was temporarily cast into prison. This only led eventually to his elevation as the overseer of all Egypt and later to a happy home and marriage. There was no "momentary slip" for Joseph—however persistent the daily temptation—and prosperity was the rich and abundant harvest for "the LORD was with him; and whatever he did, the LORD made it prosper."

These two stories show, better than words can tell, how crucial the matter of adultery is. Temptations always abound: *to succumb*, for all its seeming pleasure, *is to court death and destruction; to stand fast*, for all its seeming constraint, *is to find the way to life and true joy.*

A word should be added here about the biblical teaching on fornication—the physical relations between the *unmarried*. Although the biblical teaching on adultery does not directly include fornication, the implications are abundantly clear. To put it in the form of a question: if it is wrong for the married or unmarried to enter into relations with the married because of the great harm it does to the marriage, is it also wrong to have physical intimacy when no marriage is involved?

Granted that a person ought to be faithful to his (or her) partner *after* marriage, but is there any reason for restraint *before* marriage?

The biblical answer, in the Old and New Testaments alike, is that intimate physical relations between a man with a woman makes them "one flesh," and therefore such intimate physical relations cannot be indulged in illegally without catastrophic results.

For example: for a young woman not previously married to come into marriage not as a virgin is to bring upon herself the same penalty as for adultery: death: "If the tokens of virginity were not found in the young woman (who has just married), then they shall bring out the young woman to the door of her father's house, and the men of the city shall stone her to death...she has wrought folly in Israel by playing the harlot" (Deuteronomy 22: 20-21).

For a young man to presume that he may freely indulge in physical relations before marriage is also so quite wrong. Let us notice first the situation if the young woman he seduces is a virgin:

> *"If a man seduces a virgin who is not betrothed, and lies with her, he shall give the marriage present for her, and make her his wife."*
>
> (Exodus 22:16)

In other words, the physical act is tantamount to marriage: it cannot be indulged in promiscuously. If marriage does not follow, the act is a perversion of nature, and the man has committed fornication while the woman has lost her virginity.[10] If the physical relation is not with a virgin, but one who is "playing the harlot," he becomes "one body" with her: "Do you not know that he who joins himself to a prostitute becomes one body with her? For, as it is written, *'The two shall become one.'*" (1 Corinthians 6:16)

Any future marriage for the young man is corrupted: he cannot offer himself to a wife without bringing a prostituted body. He can never really be "one flesh" with a wife—with all the joy and wonder that contains—because a harlot stands between them.

Fornication, therefore, proves to be no less an evil than adultery. Adultery *perverts the marriage relationship after it has been established; fornication perverts it before.* They are both sinful in their destructive nature. Jesus links them together by saying:

> "For out of the heart come evil thoughts, murder, *adultery, fornication,* theft, false witness, slander."
>
> (Matthew 15:19)

Fornication, even as adultery, brings *death in its wake*: it *kills a person's future* marriage, *destroys their inner integrity,* and *shuts them off from the presence of both God and eternal life.* Regarding this latter point, one thinks of the tragic scene of fornicators and other wrongdoers standing outside the "city of God" (heaven) in the Book of Revelation. After quoting, "Blessed are those who wash their robes, that they might have the right to the tree of life and that they may enter the city by the gates," the writer must add:

> *"Outside are the dogs and sorcerers and fornicators and murderers and idolaters, and everyone who loves and practices falsehood."*
>
> (Revelation 22:14-15)

Fornication brings death—initially and for eternity. Adultery, in the second place, *may be committed through re-marriage after a divorce.*

Against the background of the Genesis picture of marriage as a high and holy relationship in which a man and woman become one flesh, divorce would seem to be unthinkable. However, divorce is permitted in the Book of Deuteronomy if a wife "finds no favor" in her husband's eyes through his discovery of "some indecency" in her. He may then write her "a bill of divorce" (see Deuteronomy 24:1-4).

With the opening of the New Testament, Jesus makes it quite clear that this permission of divorce is by no means ideal. It was sanctioned only because of people's "hardness of heart"; husband and wife in wedlock are one and nothing should pull them apart:

> *"For your hardness of heart he (Moses) wrote you this commandment. But from the beginning of creation, 'God made male and female.' For this reason a man shall leave his father and mother and be joined to his wife, and the two shall become one. So they are no longer two but one. What therefore God has joined together, let not man put asunder."* (Mark 10:5-9)

What if divorce does occur because of peoples' "hardness of heart," and one or both parties re-marry? The answer: *any newly contracted marriage is adultery.* Reading on in Mark:

> *"And he said to them, 'Whoever divorces his wife and marries another, commits adultery against her; and if she divorces her husband and marries another, she commits adultery.'"*
>
> (Mark 10:11-12)

In other words, although divorce may be tolerable because of hard-heartedness, re-marriage later is impossible because of the previous union. It is a *tragic* thing to see two people, having become "one flesh," trying to live separate lives because of divorce; but it is an *evil* thing to see either or both of them trying to contract another marriage. It is evil, indeed perverted, because the original marriage had made two people one. Man had become *man-and-wife*; *how can he who is still man-and-wife marry another without adulterating his own relationship and the life of the person to whom he marries?*

Clearly then, the Seventh Commandment may be broken just as much through re-marriage after a divorce as through extra-marital relationships during marriage. Indeed, it may be said that the commandment can be even more grievously broken through re-marriage since, rather than an occasional extra-marital act, it now becomes a rule of life.

It may be asked, what if, in the marriage, only one partner proves to be unfaithful. Are there not Scriptural grounds for a legitimate re-marriage of the innocent party? The answer to that question is "Yes," based on the parallel passage to Mark 10:11-12 (quoted previously) found in Matthew 19:9: "And I say to you: whoever divorces his wife, except for unchastity, and marries another, commits adultery." Re-marriage and not committing adultery is possible if the divorce resulted from "unchastity." *The one who has remained chaste may re-marry without committing adultery.*

Let us look at why this provision is made.[11] Bearing in mind that unchastity may refer to either fornication (pre-marital unchastity) or to adultery (marital unchastity), the reason is clear. For example, if a man discovers at marriage that his wife has been *unchaste before marriage*, he has the right to divorce her since she cannot really become "one flesh" with him; she actually became "one flesh" earlier through fornication.

Divorce in this case is a recognition that no true marriage can be entered into since the wife has "played the harlot." Divorce becomes therefore the annulment of the impossible; marriage cannot be consummated. (This case is quite similar to the one previously cited from Deuteronomy 22, where the "tokens of virginity" were not found).

On the other hand, if a man discovers that his wife is *unchaste during marriage*, he has the right to divorce her because she is really no longer "one flesh" with him: she is polluting their "one flesh" elsewhere through adultery. Divorce, in that event, is a recognition that no true marriage can be carried on, since the wife is "playing the adulteress." Divorce again becomes the annulment of the impossible: a marriage that cannot be continued.

We referred to a man's rights in case of unchastity in the wife, since the quotation from Matthew 19:9 concerns his divorce and re-marriage. However, it would surely follow that if things are reversed and the husband is guilty of unchastity, the wife may divorce him and re-marry without committing adultery,

Unchastity is, therefore, an abominable evil because it *destroys* the high and holy bond of marriage. Unchastity before marriage makes true marriage *impossible to consummate*; unchastity during marriage makes true marriage *impossible to continue*. What God has joined together man has put asunder. The evil of unchastity is vast and deadly indeed. Is it a wonder that the unchaste, fornicators and adulterers alike, deserve only the wrath and judgment of God?

Thank God; for the innocent there is a way out! No one likes divorce, but it is provided—and the possibility of a new life in a true marriage.

Now to summarize this New Testament teaching on re-marriage after a divorce: *If a man and a woman are "one flesh" in marriage* (in other words truly married), then *for both divorce is a tragedy and re-marriage an evil: the evil of adultery*. It is adultery both for the one re-marrying and the one either he or she marries.

As a result, we have Scriptures such as: "Whoever divorces his wife and marries another, commits adultery against her; and if she divorces her husband and marries another she commits adultery," and other passages such as: "Everyone who divorces his wife and marries another commits adultery, and he who marries a woman divorced from her husband commits adultery" (Luke 16:18).

If, on the other hand, two people are not "one flesh" in marriage—because one partner previously acted "unchastely"—then for the innocent party divorce is permitted and re-marriage is possible.

This is why those Scriptures are quoted: "And I say to you: whoever divorces his wife, except for unchastity, and marries another, commits adultery," and "But I say to you that everyone who divorces his wife, except on the ground of unchastity, makes her an adulteress; and whoever marries a divorced woman (one who divorced her husband not on the ground of unchastity) commits adultery" (Mathew 5:32).

Marriage is a holy and sacred bond where, through the grace of God, a man and a woman can share the mystery and wonder of being "one flesh."

How vast an evil if unchastity should pervert its consummation or continuation! How serious God's judgment is upon the unchaste, fornicators and adulterers alike; those who destroy righteousness! How rich God's mercy is to the innocent ones; mercy which allows them a way out of an unholy union and the chance to find a future marriage with holiness and true joy.

Adultery, finally, may also *be committed through other forms of lust*.

We now come to the most serious consideration of all: the whole matter of adultery as being a sin, not only of outward unchastity, but also of inward thoughts and feelings. Notice the words of Jesus in the Sermon on the Mount:

> *"You have heard that it was said, 'You shall not commit adultery.' But I say to you that everyone who looks at a woman lustfully has already committed adultery with her in his heart."*
>
> (Matthew 5:27-28)

As we have observed, Jesus reinforces the teaching in Genesis regarding marriage as being a high and holy union where two people become "one flesh." Adultery and fornication, therefore, are heinous evils because they destroy marriage: they tear asunder, they kill off the highest fulfillment of God's creation. Here we also note Jesus making clear that this destruction is not confined only to the outward act, but may also be caused through lust in the heart. This lust can even destroy the highest and the best, no one is exempt.

Perhaps it is a shocking thing to realize how destructive this power of lust is: that death can enter into a marriage relationship, not only through some outward act of adultery, but also through an inward feeling of lust. A husband, for example, may be perfectly "faithful" to his wife outwardly and yet allow lustful thoughts for other women to lay hold of his mind and heart. The wife also, for example, may be perfectly faithful to her husband outwardly and yet allow lustful desires for other men to lay hold of her mind and heart. These are both cases of adultery—and something dies in his or her marriage.

When thoughts and feelings are dissipated elsewhere, when other "flesh" becomes an allure and a desire, then their "one flesh" suffers. Its purity has been adulterated through this diffusion of passion, and they are driven apart.

Any married couple, realizing this fiendish power of lust, should seek, almost desperately, to steer clear of feelings towards others because such feelings take the "edge" off and debilitate what should be an increasingly joyous relationship within their own marriage. God made man and woman so that the two can become one in an increasingly thrilling way. The more *all* desire and passion are directed toward each other—and nowhere else—the more wonderful that relationship will become.

Many people believe that Christianity is repressive because it insists upon marriage to only one person and, also, that it checks and confines natural desires and takes some of the *fun* out of life. The truth is just the contrary:

Christian faith, the Ten Commandments, the teachings of Jesus—name what you will—is concerned that people find an even higher joy. This is because Christianity recognizes that a man and a woman never really become one, with all the happiness, delight, and ecstasy that true faithfulness contains, if their physical feelings are allowed to be drained off and scattered in many directions.

How pertinent the words of Jesus are then following His statement, "But I say unto you that everyone who looks at a woman lustfully has already committed adultery with her in his heart":

"If your right eye causes you to sin, pluck it out and throw it away; it is better that you lose one of your members than that your whole body be thrown into hell. And if your right hand causes you to sin, cut it off and throw it away: it is better that you lose one of your members than that your whole body go into hell."

(Matthew 5:29-30)

If your roving eye leads you to gaze upon others lustfully, stop it! If your roving hand leads you to touching others with desire, stop that also! This is adultery—and adultery simulates hell: destroying the heights of marriage, the depths of one's own soul, and the abiding presence of God.

Being human, every married man and woman will certainly be tempted, at times, to lust with either their eyes or hands. The world abounds with such temptations: lurid advertisements, television, movies, styles of dress designed, quite often, for the purpose of provoking lust, etc, etc. Even if so many outward temptations were not around, lust is often ready to spring up and burn in the heart of a perfectly innocent person. Temptations come, but—and this is important to realize—they do not have to lead to sin. Jesus Himself was tempted again and again, and this must have included lust (since He was human and "one who in every respect has been tempted as we are" (Hebrews 4:15); but He, though tempted, never yielded to the sin.

Now, we ask: when actually does the temptation to lust actually become sin, and therefore adultery? The answer: the very moment anyone succumbs to the temptation, consents to it in their heart, and indulges it in their feelings. Whether any outward act is perpetrated or not, adultery has been committed, and something dies.

An unmarried person may perhaps find his temptation to sin more pronounced in the direction of fornication. Desire is natural, and it may be especially strong before marriage: so desire may very easily become lust and, if directed to another unmarried person, this lust itself is fornication. Lusting is destructive because once gain it means *in spirit* to become "one flesh" with the person lusted for—and because the highest joy and happiness in life, a person can become "one flesh" with only one person in their lifetime. All lust, therefore, is deadly because it destroys much of the wonder, beauty, holiness, and joy of a man and a woman becoming one.

Now the question really is: how can we avoid lust—and all its evils? The answer is: *there is always a temptation that comes first*, a kind of warning sign. When it comes, turn away quickly from the temptation itself. If it is a lurid advertisement; refuse to enjoy it. If it is a "shady" story or joke, do not even listen to it. If another person tries to arouse your passions, refuse to pay any attention. And through it all, whatever or whomever comes, pray for God to give you the strength to never succumb, so that you can keep your mind and heart clear and free. Also we have the words of Scripture which say:

"No temptation has overtaken you that is not common to man. God is faithful, and He will not let you be tempted beyond your

strength, but with the temptation will also provide a way of escape, that you may be able to endure it." (1 Corinthians 10:13)

It is sad to think of, but what if we do fail and lust does spring up in our hearts? Then are not we all adulterers and fornicators? Yes, we are—all of us. So do you and I truly (do we really dare ask?) deserve death? Yes, we do; all of us. We have broken God's law, and the penalty for this is death. If Christ had not said that lust itself was adultery, some of us might escape because we have not outwardly committed adultery, either through extra-marital affairs or re-marriage after an un-Scriptural divorce. However, with lust included, we all stand at the same low level—we are all *adulterers and fornicators* and deserve nothing but death.

Is there not any hope?

Are we all really lost?

No, thank God. Because of Jesus Christ, we are not lost forever: *there is salvation*. Always remember: however horrendous our sins are, they can be forgiven through Christ, and all of us can have a new beginning. Remember the story of the woman caught in the act of adultery and brought into the presence of Jesus. Her accusers were ready to put her to death; and Scripturally she really did deserve it. But our Lord looked at their hard faces and said, "Let him who is without sin among you be the first to throw a stone at her." Slowly they slipped away, none of them being willing to condemn her; and then Jesus, full of compassion and forgiveness, said to the woman, "Neither do I condemn you; go, and do not sin again" (John 8:1-11).

This then is the true Gospel: the "good news" of the grace of God; the wonder of God's forgiveness to those who are truly penitent. Whatever our sin, or sins, of unchastity have been: if we have physically committed adultery and brought death into our marriage, if we have been divorced and re-married, but not on the grounds of the Scripture; even if we have burned with lust again and again, *if we are truly sorry, God, for Christ's sake, will always forgive. He will purify everything: our sinful selves, lives, and marriages. He will also help us start life all over again.*

Truly, it is God's desire, not that adulterers and fornicators be shut out of the heavenly city, but that everyone be forgiven and cleansed; so that marriage may again be what God intended it to be at creation's dawn: one man saying to one woman:

"This at last is bone of my bones and flesh of my flesh."
(Genesis 2:23)

Notes and Meditation:

The Eighth Commandment

"You shall not steal."

We are now ready to consider the Eighth Commandment, "You shall not steal." This is a commandment that, if not thought through seriously, could cause us to think:

"There's no definition needed, doesn't everybody already know what stealing means?"

An example of this is that the dictionary defines stealing partially as: "to appropriate to oneself furtively or secretly." Someone might ask, "What's the point of such wording? It just makes something simple seem complicated." Therefore, we will not really try to define what stealing is, but instead will ask what is forbidden when we are told not to steal: what are some of the penalties and, finally, what is involved in the many different kinds of stealing.

In the Old Testament, the first reference to any form of stealing is the stealing of humans and its penalty. This is found in Exodus 21:16:

> *"Whoever steals a man, whether he sells him or is found in possession of him, shall be put to death."*

The fact that the death penalty is used in the instance of "man" stealing refers to the theft of an extremely valuable property: a slave. Since, apparently, there is no more valuable possession than this, the penalty for "man" stealing is nothing less than death.

In the next chapter of Exodus, the opening paragraphs (22:1-4 and 7-12) deal with theft of animals and other property. For example:

"If a man steals an ox or a sheep, and kills it or sells it, he shall pay five oxen for an ox and four sheep for a sheep. He shall make restitution; if he has nothing, then he shall be sold for his theft. If the stolen beast is found alive in his possession, whether it is an ox or an ass or a sheep, he shall pay double."

In other words, when the stolen beast cannot be restored alive, the penalty is four or five-fold; if the beast itself can be restored alive, the penalty is double.

Let us look at another reference to double indemnity:

"If a man delivers to his neighbor money or goods to keep [hold for him], and it is stolen out of the man's house, then, if the thief is found, he shall pay double. If the thief is not found, the owner of the house shall come near to God to show whether or not he has put his hand to his neighbor's goods. For every breach of trust, whether it is for ox, for ass, for sheep, for clothing, or any kind of lost thing, of which one says, 'This is it,' the case of both parties shall come before God; he whom God shall condemn shall pay double to his neighbor." (Exodus 22:7-9)

We are not told here exactly how one knows that the condemnation of God is determined; the result, however, is that the person condemned must pay double for his "breach of trust."

Turning now to the Book of Leviticus, we find information about "breaches of faith" and the penalty that is given when it occurs. Leviticus 6:1-7 is very interesting because many situations are presented and a more comprehensive penalty is called for:

The LORD said to Moses: "If anyone sins and commits a breach of faith against the LORD by deceiving his neighbor in a matter of deposit or security, or through robbery, or if he has oppressed his neighbor or has found what was lost and lied about it, swearing falsely—in any of all the things which men do and sin therein, when one has sinned and become guilty, he shall restore what he took by robbery, or what he got by oppression, or the deposit which was committed to him, or the lost thing which he found, or anything about which he has sworn falsely; he shall restore it in full, and shall add a fifth to it, and give to him to whom it belongs, on the day of his guilt offering."

Notice that so far there has been almost the same penalty although, in this instance of the "breach of faith," one-fifth must be added. Of particular significance is what follows: "And he shall bring to the priest his guilt offering to the LORD, a ram without blemish out of the flock, valued by you at the price for a guilt offering; and the priest shall make atonement for him before the LORD, and he shall be forgiven for any of the things which one may do and thereby become guilty."

In this passage from Leviticus, there is a clear understanding of the broader and deeper nature of the iniquity of stealing; namely that one has sinned, not only against his neighbor, but *also against God*. Every theft is also a "breach of faith" with the LORD. Therefore, not only is restitution to the neighbor required, but it is also necessary for the person to come into the presence of the LORD and have the priest make atonement for him through a guilt offering.

Restitution is imperative, but it is not enough. No matter how much the restitution satisfies the demands of justice and how completely the thief is forgiven by his neighbor, he still inwardly carries the guilt before God for what he has done. Mercifully, God provides an escape from his guilt: the "ram without blemish" assumes the guilt, and in its dying, the thief's guilt "dies" with it. The thief is finally completely innocent, with man and God.

Theft of property, breaches of faith, and oppression of neighbors; these sins, mentioned in the Old Testament, obviously are still with us. All we have to do is listen to the TV news or glance at the daily newspaper to see the many ways the Eighth Commandment is broken by: larceny, embezzlement, fraud, extortion, graft, and so on. If we are willing to look at *ourselves*, we unfortunately must also admit to numerous failures, sins and breaches of faith.

We may, or may not, do enough wrong to bring us into court, but we often do commit theft. Here are several examples:

1. A man who is on an expense account goes somewhere and charges a meal he did not eat and "pockets the money."
2. A woman returns merchandise as "new," even after she has used it and stealing some of its value for herself.
3. A married couple fills out tax returns and deliberately overlooks certain items of income, exaggerates contributions, medical bills, depreciations, etc., thereby stealing from the government.
4. A person borrows an item with the "half-hearted intention of returning it, a book for example, but never really gets around to it. So that person steals by keeping it as if it were his own.
5. A young person in school, while taking a test or writing a paper, stealthily takes information from someone

else; in other words, he or she "just plainly" cheats, so has stolen and therefore broken the Eighth Commandment.
6. What of the employer who pays just barely enough in wages to get by, thus stealing energy and talent from his employees?
7. And how about the employees who do not give their best or use company time for their own concerns? Again, it is a breaking of the Eighth Commandment, as sadly all the examples are.

We could go on and on, adding theft to theft because we do indeed live in an evil generation. We may ask: "Aren't most of these practices just petty?" Yes, indeed, but is any sin really petty in the sight of God? Others may do the same things, but is not every sin of this type a heinous one, regardless of how many also transgress, or how insignificant we may wish our sins to look? *Any* theft of property, *any* breach of faith, *any* act of cheating, *any* false appropriation, no matter how "great" or "small" is a breach of the Eighth Commandment.

As surely as the Old Testament is God's Word, there must be *restitution* wherever restitution is possible, no matter how great the cost or humiliation. At the same time, there must be the *removal of guilt for our* sins through God's forgiveness. No, it is no longer necessary to bring a ram without blemish to die in our place; the Lamb without blemish *has* died on Calvary's cross, and our guilt can be atoned for only by His death. To make restitution and seek the Lord's forgiveness is to know release from our sin, find true joy, and peace.

Remember Zacchaeus, the tax collector who had lived by his graft, in the presence of Christ crying out, "Behold, Lord, the half of my goods I give to the poor; and if I have defrauded one of anything, I restore it fourfold." Immediately the wonderful reply of

Jesus came to Zacchaeus: "Today salvation has come to this house" (Luke 19:8-9).

So far we have looked at specific Scripture passages which deal with theft against one's neighbor. However, there is another outstanding passage which is concerned, not with the robbery of man but with *the robbery of God*. It would seem, from the tone of the passage, that no theft of man's property or goods, is as grievous a sin or receives as severe a punishment. We read from Malachi 3:6-10:

> *"For I the LORD do not change; therefore you, O sons of Jacob, are not consumed. From the days of your fathers you have turned aside from my statutes and have not kept them. Return to me, and I will return to you, says the LORD of hosts. But you say, 'How shall we return?' Will a man rob God? Yet you are robbing me. But you say, 'How are we robbing thee?' In your tithes and offerings. You are cursed with a curse, for you are robbing me; the whole nation of you. Bring the full tithes into the storehouse, that there may be food in my house; and thereby put me to the test, says the LORD of hosts, if I will not open the windows of heaven for you and pour down for you an overflowing blessing."*

The Old Testament is quite explicit that the most serious breach of trust possible is that of "tithes and offerings." It is not possible here to go into a description of the many various tithes and offerings required in the law of the Old Testament—except to say that one-tenth of all earthly goods was the LORD's:

> *"All the tithe of the land, whether of the seed of the land or of the fruit of the trees, is the LORD's; it is holy to the LORD....And all the tithes of herds and flocks, every tenth animal of all that pass under the herdsman's staff, shall be holy to the LORD."*
>
> (Leviticus 27:30,32)

Additionally, there were many offerings expected: free will, peace, votive, and others. So to hold back tithes and offerings was robbery: the robbery of God.

Do we fail here, *do we* rob God?

To be sure, since the coming of Christ, many of the Old Testament sacrifices and offerings have ceased but in no sense have we ceased to be stewards of God. The tithe of what God has entrusted to us, in material possessions, is still an excellent guide to us and by giving it we recognize God's ownership of everything we have. Can the Christian, with the joy of God's gracious gift of Jesus Christ, do *less* than the Old Testament Israelite who faithfully returned a tenth to the LORD? Surely we should do much more in tithes and offerings than any person under Old Testament bondage. Doing anything less brings back the haunting question: "Will man rob God?"

Therefore, a person can break the Eighth Commandment not only by financial mistreatment in relation to his fellowman but, most of all, in his relation to God: if he fails in his stewardship. However, if we have failed in tithes and offerings, we can never hope to make restitution to God in the same way we did to our neighbor. But such God does not require it, because He has not lost anything from us, except our hearts. If we return to Him, sincerely asking His forgiveness for our robbery in the past, and setting apart *now and from this point on* His portion, we will be relieved of our guilt and curse and be able to receive His outpoured blessings from the very "windows of heaven."

Now we move to the New Testament and look at two passages also regarding stealing. These passages will probe into some of the deeper meanings of the Eighth Commandment.

First, there is the word of John the Baptist addressed to certain soldiers: "Rob no one by violence or by false accusation" (Luke 3:14). John doubtless is thinking that it is very tempting for an army after pillaging the countryside to assume that whatever belonged to the people now belongs to the soldiers themselves. John warns against this kind of robbery, through "violence." He also warns against robbery through "false accusation." How very easy it is for anyone in the army or military to accuse somebody falsely for the sake of *so-called* justice being carried out very quickly. Surely, these words of John apply not only to soldiers but also to everyone.

It may be laid down, as a basic principle, that to accuse any person of anything falsely is to steal something from that person. Indeed, it is a breaking of the Eighth Commandment.

For example, a person accuses someone of a wrongdoing, either directly or more often behind the other person's back and in the presence of others. Perhaps the accusation is some malicious statement about that other person's motives. In so doing the accuser steals something because the other person's character has been assailed by words and no longer is he able to face people in quite the same way because something of tremendous value has been stolen from his life.

We think with sorrow about some of the past activities of Congressional investigating committees that have defamed peoples' characters, assuming they were guilty before anything had been proved. These people, in many cases innocent, must live on after this for many years, perhaps all their lives, with a shadow upon them because there were false accusations. Therefore any false accusation is a vicious evil because it steals from people and may even become character assassination.

How often did they falsely accuse Jesus again and again? They called Him many names seeking to destroy Him; trying to steal from Him His very Messiahship. They called Him a wine bibber, glutton, lunatic, blasphemer, and even a devil: they were constantly accusing Him falsely, and by doing so finally sent Him to the cross.

False accusation is one of the most vicious kind of thievery because it both diminishes and devalues. In home situations:

1. Husbands and wives may tend at times to make false accusations regarding each other. An argument is under way, and in its heat, false things are both said and implied. The argument may—indeed must—end eventually, but the tragedy is that the false accusations have taken something away: something has been stolen from their marriage.
2. A mother falsely accuses her child of some misdeed, and the child is hurt, perhaps badly because of some of his sense of inner worth and value is gone: stolen away, and perhaps never to return. How terrible an evil false accusation is and how seriously it breaks the Eighth Commandment!

Second, and of the utmost importance, are the words of Jesus in John 10:1-10 regarding Himself as "the door of the sheep." The passage includes the following:

"Truly, truly, I say to you, he who does not enter the sheepfold by the door but climbs in another way, that man is a thief and a robber....Truly, truly, I say to you, I am the door of the sheep. All who came before me are thieves and robbers; but the sheep did not heed them....The thief comes only to steal and kill and destroy; I came that they may have life and have it abundantly."

Jesus Christ states vividly and unmistakably that He is *the door to life*, and that any man who seeks "another way," or gets others to "heed" his voice, is a thief and a robber. Anyone then who does not point the way to Christ as the only door to abundant life is breaking the Eighth Commandment: "You shall not steal." And *this is the worst possible breaking of the commandment on the human level: for it is the theft of the human soul.*

Let us see how this can happen *in the home*. Children naturally want to know about both God and Jesus. They want to learn how to worship and pray. They want to learn about God's House and to love the church; they want the abundant life Christian faith can bring. But, alas, the parents do not show much interest; they themselves are not daily finding life through the doorway of Christ. They are trying to climb in another way, through the doors of success, pleasure, comfort or money-seeking; while the doorway to real living through Christ they are not using. It is not that they speak against Christ; they simply disregard Him and overlook all the things their children really need and want to know.

Soon the tragedy begins: the child's faith, eager to blossom, is gradually undermined. The parents do not obviously take it away, but stealthily like a thief or robber, they are stealing it through their example; until some day the child when coming to maturity finds that there is nothing left. As a result, faith is stolen; perhaps forever.

Sometimes it happens to young people who go off to *school* or *college*: they will find some teachers and professors who steal away their faith. Usually there is no direct attack on Christianity, but the basic attitude may be one that leaves God out of any consideration. Even, perhaps, their remarks in certain classes and courses may imply that religion is outdated, the Bible is really just like any other book, and that the student should be so open-minded as to never really believe anything. This then is no direct attack on the Christian faith, *but* indirectly and by stealth, something is being taken. Frequently even so-called *religious* courses can be the most destructive of all. These are courses where Christ is portrayed simply as a teacher and Christianity is just one religion among many others; rather than being *the* Way, *the* Truth and *the* Life. Something is stolen, and maybe faith is gone forever.

As a tragic example, observe how even *churches themselves* can be thieves and robbers. Yes, some churches also break the exact Eighth Commandment that they are supposed to support. For example: a church may go by the name of *Christian*, and yet not stress that Christ *truly is* the Son of God, the Savior of mankind. Such a church may present Christ as a great teacher, a great prophet, and a great leader, and a great example but say little or nothing about His Divinity: the fact that He is the Son of God, the Savior of the world.

There is no direct attack on the heart of the Christian faith: that Christ was God in human flesh, but just by avoiding it or by not stressing it, this kind of church may steal away a person's right to abundant life. Especially this is the case when the emphasis is made that Christ is only one among many: Buddha, Mohammad, Confucius, etc.; also that there are many other doors to life. The church, the school or whatever the group may be, is stealing something because Jesus said and truly said, "I am *the* door; if anyone enters by me, he will be saved." Not to say that repeatedly is for any church to be like the thieves and robbers who disregard the door and seek to climb in some other way. The church itself steals from people the way that leads to life both abundant and everlasting.

Finally, and most lamentable, the professing *Christian himself* can too easily be a thief and a robber by stealing from other people the desire to become Christian. Wherever his life does not evidence abundant living: faith toward God, hope in the future, real love for people, and living that shows the touch of Christ upon it; then he is standing and barring the door, impelling them to try climbing into life some other way.

Do we steal Christ from people?

Do we rob them of their very yearning to find His Kingdom by the kind of life *we live*?

As we come to the conclusion of our consideration of the Eighth Commandment, who cannot be almost overwhelmed with the realization of the many ways we break God's holy law. We have stolen again and again: sometimes the property and goods of others, sometimes their reputation and character, sometimes their very right to life itself. We have stolen, yes, even from Almighty God.

Thank God there is a Gospel, however: the good news spoken long ago to a thief very much like ourselves. That word to him, of broken and contrite heart, is the word we also can rejoice to hear: "Today thou shall be with me in Paradise."

Notes and Meditation:

The Ninth Commandment

"You shall not bear false witness...."

"You shall not bear false witness against your neighbor." The Ninth Commandment says this in Exodus 20:16. Immediately we find ourselves asking, "What exactly can be the meaning of this law?" Three chapters later, in Exodus 23, the first definition is given in (verses 1-3 and 7-8):

"You shall not utter a false report. You shall not join hands with a wicked man, to be a malicious witness. You shall not follow a multitude to do evil; nor shall you bear witness in a suit, turning aside after a multitude, so as to pervert justice; nor shall you be partial to a poor man in his suit....Keep far from a false charge, and do not slay the innocent and righteous, for I will not acquit the wicked. And you shall take no bribe, for a bribe blinds the officials, and subverts the cause of those who are in the right."

These verses all support the sacredness and integrity of the "Christian" judicial system. To bear false witness is defined in Exodus as:

1. To commit perjury: "to be a malicious witness." Sworn to tell "the truth, the whole truth, and nothing but the truth," the witness, instead, may speak maliciously without remembering or regarding his oath.

2. To be swayed by a mob spirit; to almost unwittingly "follow the crowd" and begin to witness falsely: "turning aside after a multitude, so as to pervert justice."

3. To be partial: "nor shall you be partial to a poor man in his suit," or else you may be tempted to bear witness falsely in his favor; while he, in fact, may not be presenting himself honestly.

4. To take a bribe: "and you shall take no bribe, for a bribe blinds." Whoever accepts a bribe is being paid to bear false witness: paid to break the Ninth Commandment. The bribe blinds because the guilty person may soon, trying to ease his conscience, begin to believe what is really false. So, he bears false witness and hurts himself. In addition—and even worse—justice is spurned and the cause of the righteous is subverted:

"You shall not bear false witness against your neighbor" is then obviously basic to the integrity of the original judicial system. Our question today therefore should be: is the Ninth Commandment still needed in modern courts of law, or did it apply only to Israel over 3000 years ago?

Fortunately, the answer is that there is really nothing outdated or outmoded in the words of Exodus 23. Perjury, mob spirit, partiality, bribery: they are exactly the same evils that still pervert today's justice system. If this is indeed the situation, why does it happen? Why is the Ninth Commandment broken so often in our courts of law? For one thing, the atmosphere is often highly charged with a strong lack of concern for *truth*. Since the basic goal on the part of both prosecution and defense is to win the case, and *not* discovering the truth, the witness may feel little desire to be really honest. He may be honest, of course, but he may also feel that supporting evidence for both sides is what they want. As a result, perjury on his part is correlated with partiality on theirs. The witness, therefore, has no real reason to fear any punishment no matter what he says; especially if he senses that the room is filled with distortions, pressure, and half-truths. Where would the punishment begin and where would it end? This means, therefore, that a lawyer may find himself, if not knowingly and willfully, breaking the Ninth Commandment, often aiding, encouraging, and inciting its infraction. The lawyer may want to find evidence more than *truth*—and if he does, it is very difficult to prove there has been actual perjury committed.

Obviously there is a real challenge for today's *Christian* lawyer. If the Ninth Commandment is so flagrantly violated in courts of law, then surely he has a God-given opportunity to always try—even if it sometimes means losing a case—to witness himself, the best he can, as the truth, the whole truth, and nothing but the truth. If he does that, praying "so help me God," he is neither advocating nor encouraging perjury in anyone and also not involved in any possible subversion of justice.

Remember also, that the verses in Exodus warn about partiality, as well as perjury; because partiality, while not in itself perjury, can also easily lead to sin. The lawyer is, of course, on one side or the other: prosecution or defense, but he is there—or should be—not to win his client's case but to see that his client receives justice. To distort or conceal facts, so that he might win the case, is partiality: it is breaking the Ninth Commandment. The lawyer is bearing false witness. He may win the case, but he has lost the truth and failed his God.

Surely, there is no finer way for any Christian lawyer to serve the Kingdom of God than in his own sphere, by always striving to strengthen and uphold the Ninth Commandment. Whatever his Christian dedication is to the Kingdom of God through service in the church, his vocational dedication should be that of a *true witness* within the courts of law in our land and nation. The Christian lawyer has an imperative and important witness to make there which he alone can make. If he fails, none of his service in the church on his part will be vital and true; if he succeeds, or is diligent to be, his service in the church will also be rewarding. If he has done this, he has truly sought to put the Kingdom of God and its righteousness first for six days of the week and deserves to worship and serve both faithfully and fully on the seventh, and whenever else he is in the house of God.

"You shall not bear false witness" through perjury, partiality, mob spirit, or bribery. A lot more could be said about courts, false witnesses, etc., but we must move on, because the Ninth Commandment is concerned with much more than just our judicial process.

The Ninth Commandment is indeed concerned about *any* false witness against one's neighbor; whether in or out of court. The first such false witness we will consider is *slander*. Leviticus says:

> *"You shall do no injustice in judgment; you shall not be partial to the poor or defer to the great, but in righteousness shall you judge your neighbor. You shall not go up and down as a slanderer among your people, and you shall not stand forth against the life of your neighbor: I am the LORD."* (Leviticus 19:15-16)

The New Testament couples false witness and slander. In the words of Jesus:

> *"For out of the heart come evil thoughts, murder, adultery, fornication, theft, false witness, slander..."* (Matthew 15:19)

We now have to ask what exactly is slander?

Slander, by definition is: any false report, maliciously uttered, which tends to injure the reputation of another. If sufficiently serious, it may be labeled as libelous and become a matter for court action. The breaking of the Ninth Commandment does not, however, have to be proven in court. Any purposely false report regarding another is slander, therefore: bearing false witness is an infraction of the Divine law.

Every four years when our two national conventions, the Democrat and Republican, are held, it is indeed fascinating to listen and watch. Yet it is also appalling to behold the tremendous amount of false witnessing regarding the opposite party. Slander may seem too strong a word—or is it really?—but again and again there is disregard of facts, distortions of truth, demagoguery, and vilification of any person on the opposing side: all for the sake of winning. Not truth but victory is the goal, and false witnessing abounds: all the "bad" is on the opposition's side, all the "good" is on the side of the party that is talking. This should not be in a Christian nation. "You shall not bear false witness." Do I, do you break this commandment through a "party spirit"?

"Now the works of the flesh are plain: immorality, impurity, licentiousness, idolatry, sorcery, enmity, strife, jealousy, anger, selfishness, dissension, party spirit....I warn you, as I warned you before, that those who do such things shall not inherit the Kingdom of God." (Galatians 5:19-21)

But let us leave law and politics now and recognize that whether or not we have ever been in a court of law or had a political thought, we nevertheless have grossly broken this commandment. We have been considering slander; so what about it, do we ever slander anyone and by doing so bear false witness? The answer, we must admit, is far too often, "Yes."

Slander, as we know, is usually spoken when the object person is not around. In a group, or with another person, the outside party is criticized and maligned: "whittled down to size." His or her motives are questioned and various insinuations are made; flaws looked for and found here and there, all of course for the sake of "truth." Another word for slander is "*gossip*"—or, at least gossip is its twin sister. The New Testament links the two together, when wicked people are described as: "full of envy, murder, strife, deceit, malignity, they are gossips, slanderers..." (Romans 1:29-30)

Those who gossip, who spread tales with little regard for the facts, are hurting others and are most definitely breaking the Ninth Commandment.

Why do we, so easily and readily, indulge in slander, gossip, and insinuation, to which we should also add scoffing, ridicule, and misrepresentation? The answer must be our own selfish desire to be the center of attention. Slander springs from jealousy, envy, ambition, and a lack of true love for others. Why do we not apply the Golden Rule? Would we indulge in slander if we actually "did unto others as we would have them do unto us"? If we ever begin to love our neighbor as ourselves, could we bear false witness in so very many ways?

Slander is such a dirty business: first of all, it defiles the person doing it. Remember the words of Jesus quoted earlier: "Out of the heart come evil thoughts, murder, adultery, fornication, theft, false witness, slander." To which He added: "These are what defile a man." A person simply cannot indulge in slander, in any form, without feeling dirty inside and appearing a little "corrupt" to other people. It defiles oneself, others, and one's relationship with God. "*O LORD,*" cried the Psalmist, "*who shall sojourn in thy tent? Who shall dwell on thy holy hill? He who walks blamelessly and does what is right, and speaks the truth from his heart; who does not slander with his tongue*" (Psalms. 15:1-3).

The other side of slander is flattery: another means of false witness. Flattery is false witness because it diverts attention and "puffs up the person." Perhaps it is strange that we so seldom think of flattery as a serious evil. We say: "Oh, everyone likes a little flattery," and yet it is extremely deceitful. Two versus from Proverbs are exactly to the point: "A lying mouth hates its victims, and a flattering mouth works ruin" (26:28). "A man who flatters his neighbor spreads a net for his feet" (29:5).

Flattery "works ruin" and "spreads a net" because it urges a person to think of himself more highly than he should; and with his head in a cloud, his feet begin to stumble and a fall is inevitable. It is no Christian service, therefore, to flatter: to tell a person how wonderful he is when actually he needs much changed inwardly or to praise a person's mediocre performance when actually he really needs help. Appreciation and thanksgiving are always good, but it is never right to "pour it on thick." To flatter is no better than to slander—remember how the Psalmist cried:

"Help, LORD; for there is no longer any that is godly....Every one utters lies to his neighbor; with flattering lips and a double heart they speak." (Psalms. 12:1-2)

The remark is sometimes made that to be a "Christian" is always to "say something nice" to people. In fact, this may be far from Christian wisdom—especially when another person may need the truth spoken in love, so he may recognize any needed correction in an area of his life, be more able to see himself as others do, and, as a result, live more honestly. Do not flatter, and do not receive it, unless you want "ruin and a net for your feet." Instead, let us pray with the Psalmist for ourselves and others: "May the LORD cut off all flattering lips" (Psalms. 12:3).

The final form of false witness is that of *lying*. In a sense, all that has been said regarding perjury, bribery, partiality, slander in any of its forms (libel, gossip, insinuation, ridicule), and flattery involves deviation from the truth and therefore is lying. It may be valuable to focus upon the character of lying which includes and goes beyond what has been said, yet in a more subtle but no less dangerous fashion. The Old Testament says:

"You shall not steal, nor deal falsely, nor lie to one another."
(Leviticus 19:11)

And the New Testament adds:

"Do not lie to one another, seeing that you have put off the old nature." (Colossians 3:9)

It is certainly striking and sobering to realize that lying is both the first and the last sin mentioned in the Bible. The first, in the third chapter of Genesis, is when the serpent in the Garden of Eden lies about God's commandment and tells Eve she will not die if she does eat some of the forbidden fruit. This lie is the precursor to Adam and Eve's sin and resultant fall. The last sin, in the final chapter of the book of Revelation, pictures those people who stand outside the city of God as "every one who loves and practices falsehood." "Certainly it's no surprise," someone may say, because lying is so very: prevalent, pernicious, subtle, damnable, destructive, and so much the hallmark of Satan himself.

Jesus refers (John 8:44) to the devil as "a liar and the father of lies." That he was the "father of lies" is illustrated in the Garden of Eden story in which his lie, the very first ever, led to other lies—"passing the buck," as we say. For example, when God confronted the man and woman with their sin, they both tried to shift the blame: "the woman...gave me fruit...and I ate"..."the serpent beguiled me and I ate"—and we are doing the same thing even today.

This ancient story leads to the most important point: the main reason for lying and for bearing any kind of false witness; namely, self-protection. A child, when being accosted for something he has done wrong, may point his finger at his sister, brother, playmate, or anyone he can find to accuse as the guilty party. Why? To protect himself. Parents cannot allow this, of course, and must administer some kind of punishment. And yet, are we not all guilty of lying the same way; speaking deliberate, straightforward lies—perhaps not very often—but in many devious ways?

Let's list just a few:

1. Passing the buck: to be unwilling to admit fault, and trying to lay the blame somewhere else. This, we have already noted, is a type of false witness as old as the human race.

2. Making excuses: to pretend not to be able to do something because of other commitments; which makes giving excuses plain, unvarnished lying and, in spite of being widely accepted, is a direct violation of the Ninth Commandment. In Luke 14:15-24, there is a tragic story of those invited to a great banquet—indeed, the banquet of the Kingdom of God—but "they all alike began to make excuses." The result of their untruthfulness was sad indeed: they were shut out forever and others took their place. It is the same even today; making excuses and all forms of lying keep anyone from the presence of God now and eternal life later.

3. Exaggeration and misrepresentation: to take facts and exaggerate or misrepresent them for the sake of winning an argument or making oneself look good. All this kind of distortion is vicious because it is a mixture of truths and half-truths and the person indulging in it moves this way and that—like a serpent—making it hard to separate the true from the false. How wonderful it is that Christ warned us, "Let what you say be simply 'Yes' or 'No.'" (Matthew 5:37)

4. False promises: to make a promise and then not keep it is also to bear false witness. For example: it is easy for a parent to promise a child something and then forget about it; or for people to take a church vow, as in baptism, and never live up to it. This kind of thing is truly evil, and clearly breaks the Ninth Commandment.

We could keep going but it all actually just adds up to self-protection and a lack of basic honesty. We live in a world full of this kind of thing. But any *true* Christian certainly must not participate: if he does, he denies the LORD he loves.

One more thing should be added because—even though it does not exactly come under "lying"—it is definitely a way of bearing false witness, namely: failure to speak out for the cause of righteousness. If a person sees an evil, hears or experiences one, and does not expose it, then he or she is bearing false witness. By failing to act or speak out, they are giving an indication of consenting to the sin. When profanity is being used, could a Christian dare to break the Ninth Commandment by remaining silent about it? If lascivious literature is on the newsstand, and indecent advertising is on TV and elsewhere, how can a Christian remain silent? If graft is seen on the job, or false advertising claims are being made by the company, can a Christian remain silent? Again we could keep going: it is so much easier not to bother and just not say anything; but there again, that is bearing false witness.

Sadly, the fact is that whenever we fail to stand for Christ in the world, gladly acknowledging His name and Lordship, we are being false witnesses and breaking the Ninth Commandment. The Scripture in Mark 14:53-72 describes a dark picture of false witnesses who maliciously distorting the facts about Christ, even while He was on trial for His life: "For many bore false witness against him" (Mark 14:56).

Even darker and more deplorable is the scene when Simon Peter bears false witness by claiming that he never even knew Jesus. We say, "But we would never do what Peter did"; yet do we not indeed do it every time we fail to speak out for Him? What happens when we say or do something that testifies actually that we do not really know Him? Jesus said, "You are my witnesses." We cannot avoid it: we are either true or false, for Him or against Him. Finally, there cannot be any greater evil than to bear false witness against Christ, especially when He died for and summoned us to be His examples to the whole world.

"You shall not bear false witness against your neighbor." Please, LORD, forgive us and help us from this day forward to follow this holy commandment better and more. Amen.

Notes and Meditation:

The Tenth Commandment

"You shall not covet...."

Coveting is a terrible evil, as two stories in the Bible show clearly. The first is found in Joshua 7.

The city of Jericho has just fallen to Joshua and the Israelites, a marvelous victory which God gave them. God immediately commands everything in the city to be destroyed except: the silver, gold, vessels of bronze and iron, and other devoted things which must be put into the treasury of the house of the LORD. If any Israelite should take anything from the city for themselves, God tells them through Joshua, that then they themselves will bring destruction upon the whole camp.

One man named Achan, however, breaks the ban by secretly taking some of the devoted things for himself. As a result, the anger of the LORD burns fiercely against the people of Israel, and soon they are defeated in battle with many people losing their lives.

In grief and despair, Joshua tears his clothes and falls on his face before the LORD. He believes God has deserted Israel, which is now doomed to destruction, and that God's holy name has been desecrated.

God then speaks to Joshua, saying:

"Arise, why have you fallen upon your face? Israel has sinned; they have transgressed my covenant...they have taken some of the devoted things; they have stolen, and lied, and put them among their own stuff. Therefore the people of Israel cannot stand before their enemies...because they have become a thing for destruction."
(Joshua 7:10-12)

Immediately, Joshua begins looking around Israel's camp to find who has done this sinful deed. Finally after a long process, the culprit is found to be Achan. When Joshua questions him, he replies:

"Of a truth I have sinned against the LORD God of Israel, and this is what I did: when I saw among the spoil a beautiful mantle from Shinar, and two hundred shekels of silver, and a bar of gold weighing fifty shekels, then I coveted them, and took them; and behold, they are hidden in the earth inside my tent, with the silver underneath." (verses 20-21)

"I coveted them, and took them," admitted Achan. Coveting was his sin, the evil that led to both his stealing and lying; its results were that God's great name was defamed and was defeat brought to Israel. As the story relates, it is what brought death to Achan himself: he is put to death, and all his coveted, stolen, and lied about treasures are burned and buried. Achan coveted what belonged to God: the silver and gold which were supposed to be given to the house of the LORD. The results: God's fierce anger, Israel's defeat, and Achan, plus his family and everything he owned including animals, all stoned and burned. Coveting was, obviously, a very serious act which brought ruin to many.

The other story is found in the New Testament, Luke 12:13-15. This incident is about a man who comes to Jesus and says, "Teacher, bid my brother divide the inheritance with me." Jesus, immediately sensing covetousness in the request, replies, "Man, who made me a judge or a divider over you?...Take heed, and beware of all covetousness; for a man's life does not consist in the abundance of his possessions."

Clearly, what lay behind the coveting of both Achan and the man who wanted the inheritance divided differently was a false view of life. That view is: *life consists in the abundance of things a person possesses.* Achan coveted for himself the very things of God, and the man coveted more of the inheritance than he had received. Both of the instances happened because of the great value placed on earthly goods: the thinking that the more a person has, in quality and quantity, the more he is really living and the more worth, or value, there is to his life.

This false evaluation of life which springs from covetousness, as we all know, is still with us. Indeed, even in popular speech, if someone asks, "How much is John Jones worth?" the answerer is invariably given in terms of earthly possessions, and the dollar sign is their symbol. "John Jones? Well, he's worth millions." Dollars represent possessions: the more Mr. Jones has, the more he is esteemed, and virtually idolized. People stand in awe of a person with untold wealth, villas, châteaux, jewels, riding stables, and many servants. "*What a wonderful life!*" many say, and in doing that they are acknowledging the fact that life indeed is being appraised by the abundance of a man's possessions. This false appraisal, without a doubt, is the very seed and seedbed of covetousness.

There may be covetousness in a child when he sees his playmate with a toy he does not have. Now he wants it a lot, even though he never has before. There is covetousness in a teenager when he or she sees that a friend has a car and plenty of spending money to go along with it. There is probably covetousness in most adults when they see a friend or acquaintance obtaining a larger and more lavish home, a choice club membership, an extra automobile or two, or perhaps a pleasure yacht. Indeed, it is very hard not to covet, especially when the world around us is falsely appraising such material gains as the roadway to both life and happiness.

Now, let us ask the all-important question: what actually is the great evil of covetousness? There are several answers. First: *covetousness may, and often does, lead to overt evils* such as stealing and lying. Think again about the story of Achan. His covetousness led to stealing, and he took what did not belong to him. It also led to lying; until apprehended he would not admit that he had some of the spoil among his own possessions. Achan both stole and lied, thus breaking the Tenth Commandment, "You shall not covet," which led directly to a breaking of the Eighth and the Ninth: "You shall not steal," and "You shall not bear false witness."

Second: covetousness so often leads to killing, which breaks the Sixth Commandment. Remember the Old Testament story of King Ahab who desperately coveted Naboth's vineyard. In order to secure it, he had false witnesses testify against Naboth, who finally was put to death. Coveting led to murder, to killing his own neighbor. Is not history just full of such incidents, where men and women have been murdered to: secure their possessions, to gain an inheritance, to secure their wealth? Perhaps even a novel you have read has something of the same storyline.

Third: covetousness has also led, again and again, to breaking the Seventh Commandment, "You shall not commit adultery." One of the saddest and darkest stories in the Old Testament (previously referred to in our discussion of the Seventh Commandment) is of King David and his covetousness for the beautiful Bathsheba, wife of Uriah the Hittite. David takes Bathsheba and then to adultery he compounds murder by ordering that Uriah is put in the front line of battle. It is such a tragic sequence: covetousness, then adultery, and finally murder.

Fourth: we can keep on going right straight through all the Commandments, showing how, again and again and again, they are so often broken just because covetousness still lives in people's hearts. Just think how frequently people break the Sabbath because they covet other people's success. For example, businesses open on Sundays: they are so often as "open for your convenience," which is just a thinly disguised veil to cover the real motive—the desire to get the profits somebody else has been making on those days. Coveting, therefore, leads to a breaking of the Fourth Commandment: "Remember the Sabbath day, to keep it holy."

Dishonor to parents—which is a breaking of the Fifth Commandment, may also quickly follow covetousness. It happens when a person covets someone else's social position and finding their own "Mom" and "Dad" to be a social hindrance and pretends they really do not exist. It may even be that the covetousness is for other people's possessions and, since "Mom" and "Dad" have now become an economic burden, there is a secret hope that they will soon pass out of the picture. How sad! Covetousness conceives and the parents God used to give life are unwanted; perhaps with dishonor and unhappiness being their tragic end.

Do we need to go further? All of the overt evil against God and people, which accompany covetousness, are vast and deadly, and it is no wonder that Jesus warned with great forcefulness: "Take heed, and beware of *all* covetousness" (Luke 12:15). The Apostle Paul also urges: "Covetousness must not even be named among you" (Ephesians 5:3).

Again, *covetousness leads to much hidden evil wherein, perhaps, none of the other nine commandments seem to be outwardly broken, but inwardly they are breached again and again.* Remember that the New Testament teaches that to be angry with hate or to ridicule one's neighbor is the same as killing, because these attitudes destroy the inner spirit. To slander, gossip, or flatter is the same as bearing false witness. To judge, criticize, envy or be jealous of anyone else may be the same as to steal because one is taking something away from that other person. It is a pity how many of these evils spring from covetousness, often without the covetousness even being admitted.

Unfortunately, people will sometimes express a number of these sinful attitudes toward others with greater material possessions. At one moment they may be highly critical, questioning their integrity and conduct (of course it is all being done behind their backs in a very skillful and gossipy fashion) and at another moment they may be full of fawning and flattery in their presence. All of this is obviously a sign of covetousness, jealousy, and envy, all burning in the person like a consuming fire.

There may be no lying, stealing, or killing, but how strong the hatred, jealousy, lust, and selfish desire must be to cause such terrible evil to be spewed out, seeking to destroy both the lives and inner spirit others. The venom in the lips and the poison from such very covetous hearts is ghastly in its nature and deadly in its effect.

To be sure, in terms of material wealth, covetousness is not limited only to earthly possessions. For example, it may be covetousness of somebody else's position. A man or woman may hope for advancement to a certain level, but when it is given or achieved by someone else, covetousness begins its vicious work. The other person may be at times hated, criticized, or talked about negatively; and at other times flattered, fawned upon, and favored, simply because the position of the other person is desired so excessively. It may also be that the successful person is even avoided, or that his or her name just is not mentioned because it is too painful a thing to do.

Furthermore, the question of whether the person who wants it so badly really deserves the promotion may not even be considered in the midst of all the self-centeredness that has broken out. In any event, the Christian commandment, "Love your neighbor," is completely swallowed up and lost amidst all the evils that selfish desire produces.

What has not been said before must be added now: all covetousness, whether it is for possessions, position, or anything else, not only hurts the other person (who can be criticized, maligned, flattered, or spurned; even if it does not come to outward lying, stealing, killing, etc., without being hurt?) but also hurts, and badly, the person who is doing the coveting.

Following are some examples of covetousness:

First, covetousness hurts coveters in the sense that *they cannot really appreciate or enjoy their own neighbors.* To covet what someone else has, or has achieved, is to prevent oneself from really knowing, appreciating, and loving the other person. Coveting blinds, as sin always does, because the eyes of the coveter are always looking at the position, money, or prestige of the other person which causes that other person to never really come into focus; nor can the coveter actually see the qualities of the other person.

Second, covetousness is hurtful to coveters, in the sense that *they are always honeycombed with insecurity, anxiety, fear of the future, and many other problems.* An individual simply cannot be covetous of others, with all its accompanying companions of jealousy, envy, criticism, and fault-finding, without really feeling guilty internally. The coveter, at times, feels like hiding from everybody and "calling it quits"; he or she is just so miserable through and through. Even if the person does gain the money, position, or eminence that has been coveted, whatever is gained turns into gall, and he is even more desperate than ever. Eventually there is a feeling of guilt even if a few extra material things do come his way; and since he has felt so inferior about these things for so long, now that they have come to him, he feels judged by everyone else. If he ever were promoted to a higher position, he would feel guilty again, because he has been coveting the job for so long. We certainly can see that covetousness is a vicious evil, eating like a cancer at the very heart and soul.

Third, covetousness hurts any person himself because *his own covetousness prevents him from doing a good job and from having a rich and, full life.* God is a wonderful God, and He has given us many, many things. He has given us every talent we were born with; He has given us certain abilities; and He has also given us specific responsibilities and tasks to be accomplished during our lifetime.

The thing that God expects of us is that we finish our jobs well, which includes: that we take in stride whatever life brings to us, that we are not looking in every direction to see if we are being recognized or whether we are successful in the eyes of the world, and whether we are being paid enough for what we are doing.

It is not success that counts with God, but faithfulness.

Therefore, whether we receive monetary rewards, recognition from others, or promotion to higher positions, these, for us as Christians, should not be of vital concern. Maybe we are worth more than we are getting or maybe we are worth less; who can really say? Even to raise the question is to get the perspective all wrong, and puts us in a constant state of ineffectiveness.

If we are faithful and using our talents with devotion towards God, the rewards will come in due season because He has promised that they will. "Seek first the kingdom of God" and these other things, that you no longer covet, will be "added unto you." But even if they do not, He added, there is joy beyond measure in serving gladly and well; then strain, worry, and inner frustrations will all be gone. Any man or woman who does this will truly know what abundant living is.

A striking verse in the Book of Proverbs comes to mind, "*All day long the wicked covets, but the righteous gives and does not hold back*" (21:26). Obviously there is a difference between the wicked man and the righteous man: the wicked man is a coveter; he is constantly concerned about what he will receive; the righteous are those who, heedless of earthly gain and prominence, give of themselves and possessions freely and do not "hold back." They give gladly, without restraint, and are a joy to those around them and, indeed, to the whole world.

Is there not something wonderfully liberating about the Tenth Commandment? It is the commandment which, if obeyed immediately, brings a rich harvest of joy. Many other commandments such as, "You shall not kill," "steal," "commit adultery" and so on, are completely negative; they do not bring joy directly when they are observed. With the Tenth Commandment, however, it is completely different; *not* coveting immediately brings about peace, happiness, and fruitfulness. The strain is gone and a person is free to really begin living.

"Oh, no," someone cries, "How can I possibly obey? I've coveted for so long that I really don't know how to stop. I know that I shouldn't covet, but knowing how to stop is an entirely different thing." Indeed, knowledge is one thing, and the power to do what one knows is another. For example, to tell an alcoholic, "You shall not drink," is really useless, unless there is some way found to help the person to stop. That he or she should not drink is something the person knows already, but the enabling power to stop drinking means the person must somehow find sufficient strength to be able to stop. If that is true of the alcoholic, how drastically true is it of a man or woman laden with covetousness. Covetousness is so deeply embedded in the human heart that no one can stop it simply through one's own will power.

It does not matter how often it is that we hear the Tenth Commandment or how frequently we read the words of Jesus, "Take heed and beware of all covetousness"; or listen to the words of Paul, "Covetousness must not even be named among you." It does not matter how often we hear or know these words, in our own strength we are still bound to fail.

Is there any hope? Is not there any way out of this terrible evil?

Indeed there is a way out, but it only happens when we, first of all, admit our own powerlessness to win the battle. Even Paul who said that "covetousness must not even be named among you," admits, in Romans 7, that he had a very difficult struggle with this very sin. Even worse, the more he tried not to covet (to live up to the Tenth Commandment) the more he coveted, "sin, finding opportunity in the commandment, wrought in me all kinds of covetousness" (verse 8). He goes on to add, quite painfully:

"I do not understand my own actions. For I do not do what I want, but I do the very thing I hate....I can will what is right, but I cannot do it." (verses 15, 18)

Immediately, almost in desperation, Paul cries out words of agony and pain, like the words of abandonment of our Lord from the cross, by saying, "Wretched man that I am! Who will deliver me from this body of death?" Paul has reached rock-bottom. Covetousness is all through him; it cannot be willed away, and neither can he live with it any longer because, like all sin, it is a thing of death and destruction. Is there any hope? "Who will deliver me...?" Then comes the resounding note of joy—there *is* deliverance—and Paul cries exultingly, "Thanks be to God through Jesus Christ our Lord!" (verse 25)

Oh, good friends, are we also like the Apostle Paul? Is covetousness a thing that is wreaking havoc in our lives and in the lives of others that we hurt? Now let us hear the good news: there is deliverance through Christ and Christ alone, if we really want it and are ready to confess our sins and look to Him for salvation. Even Paul who said in dismay, "I can will what is right, but I cannot do it," triumphantly declares elsewhere, "I can do all things in Him who strengthens me" (Philippians. 4:13). There, indeed, is the answer.

All the necessary power is in Christ and not in us. However, the power of Christ can only begin to flow through our lives when we humbly and sincerely say, "O Christ, Son of the living God, I have failed, and I will fail again and again. I have coveted, and through my covetousness I have done all kinds of evil to You, my neighbor, and to myself. As hard as I try, I cannot possibly quit so; O God, for Christ's sake, please forgive my sin. Cleanse me of my evil, and live in me. Let my coveting change to giving, and my despair to joy."

Can we pray that prayer with sincerity and will we really mean it? To pray something like this in earnest is to have the power of covetousness broken within your heart.

Even though the remnants of sin will plague us even to death's door, Christ, in us, has the upper hand. This does not mean that the struggle is all over, as though we do not have anything to do for ourselves, far from it. Rather, Christ, in us, will lead us to triumph, if we look constantly to Him in every trial we still must go through. The victory, however, is assured for: He *is* the Captain of our salvation.

"You shall not covet."

Yes, LORD, we shall not, if You are our strength and our life both now and always.

Notes and Meditation:

About the Author

J. Rodman Williams

A Phi Beta Kappa graduate of Davidson College with a Th.M from Union Theological Seminary in Virginia, J. Rodman Williams was subsequently ordained in the Presbyterian Church and served as a chaplain attached to the First Marine Corps on Okinawa and in China during World War II. During the many following years, he was a college professor, a church pastor, a professor of theology at a Presbyterian seminary in Texas, then another seminary in California, and lastly a professor in the school of divinity at Regent University in Virginia.

Williams authored many books, his magnum opus being a three volume work entitled *Renewal Theology* (Vol. 1: *God, the World, and Redemption*; Vol. 2: *Salvation, The Holy Spirit, and Christian Living*; and Vol. 3: *The Church, the Kingdom, and Last Things*. The three volumes are presently published as one unabridged volume entitled *Renewal Theology* (Zondervan, 1996).

For further information, see the website: renewaltheology.net

Other Books by J. Rodman Williams:

Contemporary Existentialism and Christian Faith (Englewood Cliffs, NJ: Prentice-Hall, 1965).

The Era of the Spirit (Plainfield, NJ: Logos, 1971).

The Pentecostal Reality (Plainfield, NJ: Logos, 1972).

Ten Teachings (Carol Stream, IL: Creation House, 1974).

The Gift of the Holy Spirit Today (Plainfield, NJ: Logos, 1980).

Renewal Theology (Grand Rapids: Zondervan, 1996)
Three Volume Set includes:

> Vol. 1: God, the World, and Redemption (Grand Rapids: Zondervan, 1988).

> Vol. 2: Renewal Theology, Salvation, the Holy Spirit, and Christian Living (Grand Rapids: Zondervan, 1990).

> Vol. 3: Renewal Theology, The Church, The Kingdom, and Last Things (Grand Rapids: Zondervan, 1992)

Recommended Reading From Corinth House Publishers:

ABRAHAM AND SARAH:
History's Most Fascinating Story of Faith and Love
by J. SerVaas Williams

MOSES AND HATSHEPSUT
by J. SerVaas Williams

SEVEN TALES OF CORINTH
by J. SerVaas Williams

End Notes

[1] The "law" here mentioned, as the context shows, includes more than the statements in the Ten Commandments. But that Christ's words refer primarily to the Decalogue is apparent from the subsequent verses 21-30. See also Matthew 19:17-19.

[2] See also Mark 12:28-31 and Luke 10:25-28 (in this latter account the words are spoken by a lawyer with Jesus' full approval).

[3] It is interesting to note that the Revised Standard Version of the Bible (from which our quotations are regularly taken) gives "besides" as an alternative translation. See marginal reference on either Exodus 20:3 or Deuteronomy 5:7.

[4] Or as "Jehovah." For example, the older Revised Version of the Bible (1901) everywhere uses the term "Jehovah" for "LORD."

[5] The James Moffatt translation.

[6] "Come Holy Spirit, Heavenly Dove"—stanza 2.

[7] Tennyson's *Idylls of The King*, "The Round Table," the "Gareth and Lynette" portion.

[8] The bill was defeated in the Senate several days later.

[9] Indeed the Hebrew word "ratsach" is more accurately translated as "to murder" than "to kill."

[10] Exodus 22:17 adds: "If her father utterly refuses to give her to him he shall pay money equivalent to the marriage present for virgins." That is to say, the father can protect his daughter against an unwanted marriage but, even then, money must be paid; recognizing that an act constituting marriage has been committed.

[11] The writer is aware that some biblical scholars deny that Jesus Himself made this provision. For example: the *Interpreter's Bible*, in discussing the phrase "except unchastity," in Matthew 19:9, states, "this exception does not go back to Jesus." I feel strongly that this provision is a true expression of the Christian understanding of the meaning of marriage and the "divorcing quality" of unchastity.

Made in the USA
Columbia, SC
31 December 2017